Spiritual Growth and Personal Development

COMMUNICATING WITH YOUR SPIRIT GUIDES

MONIQUE JOINER SIEDLAK

Oshun
Publications

Communicating with Your Spirit Guides © Copyright 2021 by Monique Joiner Siedlak

ISBN: 978-1-950378-85-2

All rights reserved

The content contained within this book may not be reproduced, duplicated or transmitted without direct written permission from the author or the publisher.

Under no circumstances will any blame or legal responsibility be held against the publisher, or author, for any damages, reparation, or monetary loss due to the information contained within this book, either directly or indirectly.

Legal Notice

This book is copyright protected. It is only for personal use. You cannot amend, distribute, sell, use, quote or paraphrase any part, or the content within this book, without the consent of the author or publisher.

Disclaimer Notice

Please note the information contained within this document is for educational and entertainment purposes only. All effort has been executed to present accurate, up to date, reliable, complete information. No warranties of any kind are declared or implied. Readers acknowledge that the author is not engaged in the rendering of legal, financial, medical or professional advice. The content within this book has been derived from various sources. Please consult a licensed professional before attempting any techniques outlined in this book.

By reading this document, the reader agrees that under no circumstances is the author responsible for any losses, direct or indirect, that are incurred as a result of the use of the information contained within this document, including, but not limited to, errors, omissions, or inaccuracies.

Cover Design by MJS

Cover Image by barunka262@depositphotos.com

Published by Oshun Publications

www.oshunpublications.com

Contents

Other Books in the Series	v
A Great Offer	vii
Newsletter Sign Up	ix
Introduction	xi
1. We All Have Spirit Guides	1
2. How We Experience Our Spirit Guides	15
3. Steps to Connect to Your Spirit Guides	27
4. Start a Spirit Guide Journal	33
5. Listen	39
6. Write With Your Spirit Guides	43
7. Ask for a Sign	45
8. Develop Daily, Weekly, or Monthly Spiritual Practices	49
9. Pay Attention to the Guidance That You Receive	55
10. Use a Divination Tool	57
11. Stay in the Energy of Gratitude	65
12. Release the Outcome and Trust in a Better Plan than Your Own	71
13. Be More Childlike	75
14. Ask Your Spirit Guides for Their Names If You Feel Called To Do So	79
15. Trust in Your Own Psychic Ability	83
16. How to Ground Yourself after Connecting With Your Spirit Guides	87
17. Spiritual Shielding and Defense	91

Conclusion	95
References	99
About the Author	105
More Books by Monique	107
Last Chance	109
Thank You!	111

Other Books in the Series

Spiritual Growth and Personal Development
Creative Visualization
Astral Projection for Beginners
Meditation for Beginners
Reiki for Beginners
Manifesting With the Law of Attraction
Being an Empath Today
Crystal Healing: A Beginner's Guide to Natural Healing

Want to learn about African Magic, Wicca, or even Reiki while cleaning your home, exercising, or driving to work? I know it's tough these days to simply find the time to relax and curl up with a good book. This is why I'm delighted to share that I have books available in audiobook format.

Best of all, you can get the audiobook version of this book or any other book by me for free as part of a 30-day Audible trial.

Members get free audiobooks every month and exclusive discounts. It's an excellent way to explore and determine if audiobook learning works for you.

If you're not satisfied, you can cancel anytime within the

trial period. You won't be charged, and you can still keep your book. To choose your free audiobook, visit:

www.mojosiedlak.com/free-audiobooks

Introduction

We live in a beautiful time. Regardless of the sociopolitical movements across the globe, there is a definite spiritual awakening and growth that has never been witnessed before. It is now common to speak about the unseen hands that guide us. It is not as taboo as before, and with this newfound power, more and more people are reaching out to learn to navigate their own spiritual landscape.

Spirit guides are all around us all of the time. There is not a single second that assistance is not right beside you. Calling the spirit is as easy as thinking a thought, projecting a feeling, and believing. Physicist Alan Lightman spoke about his experience in a boat under the enormous expanse of the night sky above the ocean's darkness. That single experience allowed him to understand that there is something sacred, something permanent, and unquantifiable about the universe, something which science has not yet been able to dissect, bottle, and tag.

The point to understand spiritual matters is that it has absolutely nothing to do with the measurement and accuracy of the world's experience. It has to do with your own personal involvement, feelings, and the life-changing after-effects of being graced by spirit. When you eventually reach the point

Introduction

of understanding that spirits exist, that you are not alone in your journey on this planet, and that you never were, you will change. You cannot awaken to spirits and not be altered in some massive way.

Many people's lives change completely. There is a sign of courage instilled inside us when we encounter the beauty of spirits. Unfathomable bravery that everything is and will always be perfect as long as we hold onto our connection with spirits. The incredible feats displayed by those who have encountered their guardian angels or have been rescued by departed loved ones are astounding, to say the least. It is no secret in this digital age that we are awakening to the presence of the otherworld spoken about in myths and tales of old. It is no secret that you are awakening to your own connection. Communicating with Your Spirit Guides has been written as a loving guide for you.

Navigating the real world is scary enough. Navigating the spirit world is an entirely different map altogether. For them to work together without fear or confusion, you must have the right hand to hold. That loving guiding hand is the hand of your spirit guides. May this book bring you closer to the spiritual assistance that has always been right with you from the very beginning and will be right beyond the very end of this world.

ONE

We All Have Spirit Guides

A SPIRIT GUIDE IS DEFINED AS A DISCARNATE BEING ASSISTING an incarnated human being in this physical realm (Wikipedia, 2020). Spirit guides can range from angels, passed on loved ones, humans who have chosen the enlightened path and returned to help humanity, deities, as well as the animal kingdom.

Spirits are not shy when choosing a wide array of symbolism to connect with us. We are so detached from the reality of spirituality that we often forget the expanse of the spiritual landscape. It is a shamanic understanding that the modern human cannot juggle both the enormity of spiritual knowledge and the hustle and bustle of present-day life.

For this reason, we need not all become religious or spiritual leaders, shamans, or venture into the wilderness to embark on a spiritual study. Instead, we may simply learn to connect with our spirit guides and meander through the real world with far more ease and comfort. To learn to communicate with our spirit guides, it is essential to understand the central guides that exist. These are those guides who have been documented time and time again.

Archangels

Archangels have been documented throughout time across the entire globe. The word archangel comes from the Greek words for arch and angel, which translates to "angel of origin" or "chief angel."

The religion is known as Zoroastrianism, one of the oldest, continuously practiced religions to date. Mentions six "holy immortals" referred to or revered as archangels. These angels differ significantly from the Abrahamic traditions, where, according to the Book of Enoch, we find seven holy angels (Charles, 1917). The archangels are many and are found across cultures and religious sects. You'll find many archangels have been called various names. Many have been known as previous deities, gods and goddesses, and have been mainstreamed into religions.

In today's spiritual movement, it is more generally accepted, without the confines of religious law, but of spiritual liberty. We have five main archangels who do interact with and assist on behalf of humanity. These archangels are Metatron, Gabriel, Michael, Uriel, and Raphael.

Archangel Metatron is known as the chief of all archangels and spiritual intercessors. It is rumored that Metatron was the prophet, Enoch. He ascended to heaven to become the chief angel of The Presence. Many spiritual leaders and guides, especially those in the New Age Movement, attest to the presence of Metatron being experienced by a brilliant, almost blinding flash of light.

Archangel Gabriel is one of the only archangels to be believed to be female. She is a divine protector of writers and poets, artists, and creatives alike. Gabriel is frequently described as embodying a rose-colored aura and is rumored to be responsible for the genius ideas popping into one's head. However, this incredible gift is shared by another lesser-known archangel, archangel Raziel. Gabriel is also the messenger of

God and will visit in dreams as well as the waking state. Interestingly enough, it is Archangel Gabriel who revealed the Quran to Prophet Muhammad. It is also Gabriel who, in the Christian bible in Luke 1:29, announces to Mary that she will mother Jesus Christ.

Archangel Michael is the protector of humanity. Almost always depicted in a blue hue. All instances of him in art have carried this blue association with them, often including his shield and sword, other times showing him with scales. Archangel Michael is known as the protector of all and listens to every petition for protection and safety and being a psychopomp for those who pass over. Michael shares this duty with another archangel known as Azrael. Archangel Michael is also the guardian and shield of those who have been victims of sexual abuse or believe they are in danger. The presence of Archangel Michael has been recorded across the world; however, it is more prominent in Mexico, Italy, and France (Illes, 2009). Archangel Michael is also the angel to call upon when there is negative energy or a suspected spiritual attack within one's life. Like Archangel Raphael, Michael banishes demons and harmful spirits at the request of humans.

Archangel Uriel is the archangel of illumination and enlightenment. Uriel's name means "God's Light." When he is experienced, it is usually through the lighting of a specific area that was troubling or a significant lift in one's own spirit. Archangel Uriel is hardly described as a physical angel. In many instances where Uriel's presence is experienced, and straightforward messages have come through, the clairvoyant's presentation will describe a brilliant shining light. It is not that Uriel does not have a form. It is simply that it is not witnessed as often as the other angels' are. Uriel is also a brilliant guide through times of darkness. It has the ability and the inclination to lift those who find themselves in a state of depression or a place of no return.

Archangel Raphael is the healer of all, the great

archangel who has traversed the great holy books throughout time. Raphael is the compassionate one, the lover of humankind, and the angel who provides gifts of happiness, insight, and love. Archangel Raphael protects, shields, and heals, his healing has no boundaries, and his wisdom of all healing arts is eternal. One exceptional detail about Archangel Raphael is that he is said to hold the secret of the ineffable name. With all his greatness, this archangel banishes nightmares and protects children or young adults who are leaving home for the first time.

The following ancient Hebrew prayer, which is chanted in the evening, calls for the protection of all four archangels, as well as the divine energy of the universe:

B'Shem Adonai Elohai Yisrael,
Mimini Michael, U'mishmoli Gabriel,
U'mulufinai Uriel, U'mayachorai Raphael,
V'al Roshi Shekinath El
(Crowley & Crowley, 1994)

If you prefer to utter the prayer in English, the translation of this prayer is as follows:

In the Name of the Lord, God of Israel
May Michael be at my right hand; Gabriel at my left;
Before me, Uriel Behind me, Raphael;
And above my head, the Divine Presence.

Guardian Angels

Each person has a guardian angel. Your guardian angel has been with you since your conception. It is said that there is an ethereal chord that runs from you to your guardian angel. It allows this divine being to be with you all the time, feel what you feel, and assist you wherever and whenever you require assistance. The generally documented guideline between the assistance a guardian angel can provide and that they do provide is that it must always be in line with your divine purpose here on Earth (Laurie-Elle, 2019).

While you cannot see the future or sometimes understand the past completely, your guardian angel can. If you do not ask for assistance, they may not step in and intervene. Similarly, if the guidance you ask for is not in unison with the greater plan, they can also not assist. Your guardian angel is with you to protect you and guide you always.

Guardian angels are said to be in the order of one of the Byzantine and Eastern Catholic Orthodox traditions' archangels named Barachiel. Within the study of theology, this archangel is the chief of all guardian angels and maybe petitioned when one cannot pray to one's own guardian angel. Archangel Barachiel will also connect you with your guardian angel. He can also bestow any blessings or protection on you, just as your guardian angel would have done.

Guardian angels are said to manifest their presence in a myriad of ways. From symbolic messages, radio station answers television commercials, billboard signs, ideas that pop into your head, bursts of light, and anything which allows you to feel that it means more. There is always guidance present from your guardian angel, especially when you have asked for guidance. You only need to become aware of their presence.

Spirit Animals

Animal medicine is as powerful and healing as any of the spirit guides that are there to assist us on our paths to the enlightenment of any degree. Various shamans, druids, and healers worldwide use either animal medicine, plant medicine or mineral medicine, or a combination of all three. When working with the spirit of anything, it is generally accepted to refer to it as medicine. Therefore, working with your spirit animal would be referred to as incorporating animal medicine into your life. Your animal medicine within your life comes in many different forms, sometimes it changes, and it is difficult to understand this when first starting out on the path.

A spirit animal is with you from the start of your incarnation on this planet and will remain with you until you move into the next incarnation. Your spirit animal is you in pure spirit animal form. It is an animal that is precisely your purest mirror image, so it is the image of your soul. It is important to understand that your spirit animal does not change, ever. Communicating with your spirit animal begins with learning everything you can about this animal. Surround yourself with representations of this animal and find your own truth through the healing medicine of this animal.

An animal totem is different from a spirit animal. Many animal totems may come to you throughout your lifetime. However, they come to teach their medicine to you to assist you on your path. Just like you can draw strength and attributes from your spirit animal, so too can you apply medicine into your life from your totem. The totem is usually an animal that provides you strength if you lack it, social skills if you need them, or even patience. Every single animal holds powerful shamanic medicine. No animal is precisely the same, just like no human carries the same energetic signature in life.

Any animal can be petitioned to work with, grant one specific attribute to learn, or unlearn certain aspects of oneself. For example, a black panther may be petitioned to learn courage and strength. In contrast, if the same person would like to transform their anger into patience and calm, they could use the medicine of the sloth. Using the guidance of the animal kingdom can bring great healing into one's life. However, it can also force us to look at the reality of who and what we are without question.

Ascended Masters

The proverb "When the student is ready, the master will appear" is perfect for explaining what an ascended master is. An ascended master has lived upon the Earth, other planets, or within different dimensions or star systems. By running the karmic cycle or many lives of learning, these beings evolved so far that their mastery over self and all lessons contained within all paths were attained. With this mastery of self, they ascended and had the option of not returning to assist any life forms again. However, ascended masters have chosen to return to help where they can.

On Earth specifically, we have knowledge of many ascended masters. However, many of them are grouped into those who work diligently and are easily contacted and petitioned for assistance. The ascended masters in this group are Yeshua (Jesus Christ), Kuan Yin, Thoth, Babaji, Mother Mary, Melchizedek, Saint Francis, and Yogananda. There are many more ascended masters, and an ascended master will work with you if you are in the line of service that they assist with.

Interestingly enough, many of the ascended masters from the literature found in modern society are, in fact, saints, sages, and mystics, as well as pagan gods and goddesses who favored humankind. The spiritual realm of teachers is as vast as it is diverse, and there is no harm in connecting with an ascended master. Some ascended masters, such as the Lemurian ascended master, Ra Mun, are channeled through many people who were either incarnated in Atlantis or Lemuria or have a service. His guidance is needed.

There are many ascended masters. There are also many factors contained within the realms of existence that we have not even begun to comprehend. An ascended master is identified by their wisdom of life, their forgiving personality, and their dedication to the enlightenment of the human race as a whole. An ascended master will never ask you for anything in return for their assistance.

Below is a list of the traits and generally accepted descriptions of the ascended masters mentioned above:

Ra Mun - Lemuria is a long-lost continent before the age of Atlantis. This continent was said to be filled with feminine energy, rational and nurturing. The people of Lemuria were part of what is now known as the Brotherhood of Mount Shasta. While this brotherhood has sworn an oath to the following of the teaching of Buddha, the focus of this brotherhood now lies within the realms of archangelic energy as well as that of Confucius and the seven rays of the Elohim. Their retreat is said to exist within the Grand Teton Mountain. Ra Mu or Ra Mun is a member and master of this brotherhood. Ra Mun is the feminine aspect of all creation (Norman & Spaegel, 1988).

Saint Francis of Assisi - Born to wealthy parents in 1181, Saint Francis of Assisi was only canonized two years after his death in 1228. Saint Francis was the first receiver of stigmata that was found to be authentic by the Vatican. Stigmata are the wounds of Christ the crucified that appear on highly religious devotees with no scientific explanation of their origin. Stigmata can also be pain or markings in the same areas. Saint Francis had an epiphany from God, and his life changed completely. He followed God and preached the word of Christ's teachings to animals and people alike. He is known as the protector of animal lovers and those who work with animals (Of & Backhouse, 1994).

Yogananda - Paramahansa Yogananda was an Indian yogi and monk who was born in 1893. He is responsible for bringing the teachings of yoga, especially Kriya yoga and meditation, to the Western world. His teacher, Babaji, is also an ascended master. Yogananda is very active in assisting people on their life path, whether it be on a small or large scale. His specialties lie in healing and bringing compassion and love to the world as a whole (Yogananda, 2008).

Yeshua - Yeshua or Jesus Christ is best known for being the Son of God in the Christian faith and a prophet in the Islamic faith. Yeshua works closely or in conjunction with many of the ascended masters, especially Yogananda, who had a deep reverence for Yeshua. The teachings of Yeshua preach love, compassion, and understanding on all levels, as well as the premise that belief like a child will allow you to enter the kingdom of heaven (Johnson, 2001).

Melchizedek - Mentioned in the Book of Psalms in the Christian Bible, Melchizedek belongs to an order of high-level spiritual beings who bring ancient esoteric teachings to the people of Earth. It is thought that Melchizedek could have been a second Jesus Christ. It is also surmised in the writings of the Nag Hammadi texts that he was indeed a previous or first incarnation of the spirit of Yeshua. Melchizedek is well-loved throughout the modern world and has made numerous appearances to many leaders of spiritual faiths. His name translates to "righteous king" (Lord Melchizedek, 2016).

Mother Mary - Mother Mary, Our Lady of Guadalupe, has been called the Queen of Angels, the Virgin Mary, and of course, the Mother of Jesus Christ. Her influence permeates throughout the world, and those who believe in her have profound miraculous accounts of her presence. Mother Mary is said to have lived a terribly difficult life on Earth. Still, according to some, she also ascended and became the beloved master. He heals and helps all, especially mothers and children (Illes, 2011).

Kuan Yin - Kuan Yin is the very personification of compassion. It is thought that she could once upon a time have been a man. Still, due to the thought of men being compassionate being socially unacceptable, she was transformed into the image of a woman. Kuan Yin reached Buddhahood after her own fall from the heavens when she gave up healing out of frustration. When she fell from the heavens, she realized her mistake. Her own teacher, Buddha Amithaba, was joined with her for all eternity. Goddess Kuan Yin is very active in her appearances and assistance throughout humanity. She has no judgment for those that she assists (Illes, 2009).

Babaji - Babaji was brought to the Western world by Yogananda himself. Babaji is said to have a temple deep in the Himalayan Mountain Range, which is only visible to his devotees or those of pure spirit. He is thought to be the incarnation of Lord Siva himself and being 2000 years old. Babaji holds the exact same teaching of Jesus Christ (Yogananda, 2008).

Thoth - Thoth is the Egyptian God of writing, wisdom, music, the arts, and alchemy. Thoth is known by many names including, Tehuti, Hermes Trismegistus, and A'an. Thoth is recognized in two distinct forms, that of the ibis and that of the baboon. It is thought that while Thoth was a God in the Egyptian era, he was also a priest-king in Atlantis. Thoth brings with him great wisdom and is an enforcer of great clarity to any situation (Hermes, 2002).

When working with ascended masters or any spiritual guide, remember that all the information contains something of the person transmitting the information. Much of the information is not backed by science or historical facts. If you have an academically inclined mind, then the spiritual path will be challenging to travel. This is not to say that what is contained in the spiritual teachings is false. However, it is necessary to remember to trust your own experience and your own feelings when approaching any subject in the spiritual niche.

All spiritual texts have been created by humankind. Whether it is scientific documentation or spiritual lore, every piece of writing that we have written by another human being is written. With that comes human error. It is important to look beyond human error and reach into your own being so that you can access the truth of your own spiritual experience.

Kuan Yin is a wonderful, ascended master who asks for nothing in return, Mother Mary. However, if it is wisdom and knowledge that you are after, Thoth would be the first choice. The modern world is striving for enlightenment on a mass scale never seen before on our planet. It is peculiar that two distinct paths are running simultaneously on Earth, the one of spiritual questing and moving off the grid and the other of material acquisition in all its forms. The hunt that humanity is experiencing on a deep subconscious level stems from the quest for meaning. We want to know more, do more, be seen doing it, or be given an award for our good deeds.

The hard, cold truth is that there is no end to this path. There is no award but your own healing and witnessing the healing of the world around you. Ascended masters are well aware of this fact. When approaching spirit for the wrong reasons, you must be prepared to have your life turned upside down, inside out, and redirected to align with the spiritual way. Enlightenment is not easy, nor is any spiritual practice. It requires hard work and sometimes a daunting reality check of who and what you really are. Remembering your heart's intention is key to this process, and if you have the right choices on this path, all of the spirits will be at your side to guide you.

Departed Loved Ones

When a soul passes over into the Summerlands, the void, the astral, or what you believe to be on the other side of this reality, it is thought that they have a choice to delay their reincarnation or progression along their cycle. To return and assist loved ones that they have left behind. While it is important to note that after physical death on this plain, a spirit does not possess the same emotional ties as it did in life. Still, it does contain the knowledge of those that they are connected to. One possibility for returning departed loved ones is the existence of soul clusters. Soul clusters are a collection of connected souls bound to each other. It is suggested that those who come back to assist do so because they belong to the same soul cluster, and by helping that cluster, everyone benefits.

Departed loved ones may present themselves in an array of different manners. Such as moving furniture, dropping specific photographs, touching your hair, giving you chills, or simply whispering close by. There is a massive difference between a departed loved one returning to assist you in this lifetime and what is known as a poltergeist. Or even a shadow person or any form of terrifying apparition. Departed loved ones who choose to assist have absolutely no residue emotional tie of rage, anger, resentment, or even guilt. They return purely in the spirit of service to you.

Helper Angels

Depending on the culture or religious affiliation that you are working with, angels or messengers and guardians from the heavens are placed into a specific order or even a hierarchy. According to Christian, texts we find that the angels are put into three orders or choirs. Within the three groups, you have the angels separated into nine classes. Each of the nine classes has particular duties and can perform very specific tasks. The highest of the nine classes is known as the Seraphim, and these angels are the closest to God. The archangels are thought to be seraphim.

The lowest of the nine orders is known simply as "angels," and it is in this order where we would classify the helper angels. Helper angels, according to author Tanya Richardson, are known as "freelance angels." They are highly specialized angels who wait on humanity to provide service in every area of our reality. There is nothing that a helper angel cannot assist with, from computer problems to marriage counseling. The helper angel only needs a request in thought or word, and they will be right there to help you.

On the other spectrum, helper angels can work through humanity itself and send a human who is in tune with their vibrational frequency to assist you. Instances like these appear to be coincidences, and the person who is in service is usually the most unlikely individual. Helper angels are the most accessible angels to speak to and to connect you with the angelic realm. A helper angel has a service to humanity, and this is their duty. According to Richardson, helper angels require a specific request, and it should be as detailed as possible. There is also no amount of help that you can request that will be considered too much. The helper angels are at your service every minute of every day.

TWO

How We Experience Our Spirit Guides

EXPERIENCING SPIRITS REQUIRES AWARENESS. AWARENESS IS developed through meditation and through quieting the mind and learning to live in the present moment. There is a universe of symbolic language which is assigned to certain entities. However, some people experience the same entity without the same symbols applying. This is because our culture and social experience provide us with a precise symbolic understanding. Within these confines, we attribute meaning to our experiences.

What is taught in one culture to represent death could mean life or rebirth in another culture. Our spirit guides always speak in our own symbolic language. For example, suppose you have a personal belief that snakes are the omen for evil, but your friend sees the snake to mean the same as the ouroboros. In that case, you see a snake in a dream will be a warning, where your friend seeing a snake in a dream could mean the continuation of an aspect of their life, or that something will not come to an end.

When people begin on the path of finding their spirit guides, they become extremely disheartened because they are not experiencing the same visualizations and symbols as someone else. Consequently, their experience cannot be validated. It is also very common for people to utilize general attributions to pinpoint entities. In other words, the crow symbolizes death in almost every culture across the globe, and old wives' tales even speak of the number of crows seen as being the difference between death and an extreme accident. A person who has the crow as their spirit animal will see the crow as strength, guidance, wisdom, and a message that everything is okay. Someone who then attempts to explain this vision or experience using a general symbolic interpretation will be terrified and expect something awful to happen. But there is nothing to be afraid of.

Incorrect interpretation leaves our spirit guides quite perplexed. They will then attempt to send us more signs and symbols to bring our awareness into the correct place. Using general meanings or meanings that belong to someone else can only be used as a guideline. It should never be a definite stopping point. Your intuition, your gut instinct in this matter, is imperative for the correct interpretation. The encounters that you have with your spirit guides are your own and belong to no one else. Your spiritual path contains its own messages and symbolic meanings. It is essential to make sure that everything outside of your experience is used only as a loose example for guidance and nothing concrete.

Numbers or Number Sequences

Spirits speak in symbolism. Numerology, the study of numbers being attributed to specific events in the future, past and present, is apparent in many of the number sequences communicated to you through spirit. Everywhere we look around us, numbers are present. It is one of the most straightforward modes of communication for us to become aware of. Through this awareness, it builds our own relationship with spirit.

Numbers and number sequences exist across the spectrum of our lives, whether we are aware of them or not. Not only is it apparent that spirit communicates with us in this manner, but hidden within each number. Every number sequence is a universal pattern and unwritten guidance that will only be known by you. It is important to know the difference between looking for meaning and being contacted by your spirit guides.

When the number appears "out of the blue" and catches you by surprise, and is accompanied by a feeling, you know that a message is being transmitted. It does not help to wait for 11:11 on the clock and then look up the meaning and use that as a new direction in your life. It is thought that double numbers, or repeating numbers on the clock, are a sure sign that your spirit guides are with you. However, it must be told that they are with you all the time regardless. It is not the spirit guides that need to remember us. It is us that need to remember and be aware of them.

The number 13 has been thought to be an unlucky omen, which could not be further from the truth. Count Louis Hamon, or more famously known as Cheiro, was a formidable seer who correctly predicted the death and life events of many, including Queen Victoria, King Humbart of Italy, and King Edward VII. He had also consulted many more, including Mark Twain and Dame Nellie Melba. Chiero speaks extensively on how the number 13 is more a number of power and dominion than an unfortunate omen. Many people believe that the number 13 is a sign of impending doom because it was studied to a great extent within all of the occult spheres. The number is, in actuality, the number symbolizes the change of anything in question.

Each number from one to nine is known to be about the self. In other words, these numbers, when seen, will have direct meaning and effect on the self. Below is a short description of each of the single-digit numbers.

Number One

Number one is the masculine sign of the sun. It carries with it the origin of the universe and the first conscious idea. One is a number of creation. It is the beginning of all the other numbers until nine. Number one signifies the start of a new project, the inception of something to come.

Number Two

Where number one is the sun, number two is the feminine sign of the moon. This number carries with it the meaning of all creativity and artistry. Sensitivity and intuition lie in the undercurrent of this number. In other words, when seeing this number frequently, it is a message to use your instinct on a decision or to look at how you are treating something emotionally. Are you being too sensitive, or have you placed too little emotion into the situation?

Number Three

The number three is the number of fertility, growth, and the beginning of life within this reality. It is the culmination of the masculine one and feminine two to bring complete harmony and new development within the three. The number three brings with it a new birth, not always in the sense of an actual labor, but a project or a dream that should be placed into action. Number three is also strongly connected to the planet Jupiter.

Number Four

The number four holds an array of fear and aversion. The fear of this number is known as tetraphobia and is more common in East Asian nations. The number four is thought to be unfortunate because the word for death is almost precisely the same as the number four within many of the Asian languages. For example, in Cantonese, the word for death is sei, and the number four is séi.

The number four is a number of choices and carries a very realistic approach. If the number four is being seen constantly, then the message is to choose. There is something in your life that you are slacking with, and a choice needs to be made. It is also important to note that within this choice, something must be left behind. This message coincides with the number four and its correlation with the planet Uranus.

Number Five

The number five is a number of movements and excitement. This number does not carry stability but instead craves everything fast-paced, providing an adrenaline rush. Number five is a number of adventure and flexibility. When finding this number as a form of communication from your spirit guides, look at your life and see if you are taking everything a little too seriously? Is it time to take a break? Or, on the flip side of the coin, have you been partying a little too much and working too little? Is it time to buckle down and get your ducks in a row? The number five is also associated with the planet Mercury.

Number Six

With the direct influence from its ruling planet, Venus, number six carries all the emotional ties you can think of. From family to community to friends and animals. Number six is also a number of hope and promise of affection in one's life. The number six message from your spirit guides asks you to look at the amount of emotion in your own life. Are you giving enough of yourself to everyone around you? Is there some aspect of your life that requires some more love and affection? Perhaps it is a quiet and introverted child that needs some extra attention, or maybe your community has a need that you can assist with.

Number Seven

Number seven is connected with the symbolic nature of water and of the planet Neptune. It holds great mystery and a deep connection with core religious and spiritual affiliations. Number seven asks you to look deeper into any given situation. It is also a number that begs you to review your perception and your skeptical nature towards something. Suppose you have been seeing this number often, and you are on an initiatory path in any spiritual movement. In that case, this number means that the door to the inner mysteries is open. The number seven holds a pearl of more profound wisdom on any subject. Its solitary nature must be taken into account when understanding the message given by your spirit guides.

Number Eight

The number eight is a number that stretches to the far reaches of any subject. It is the zenith of anything that it is involved in, and as a message from your spirit guides asks you to go to the nth degree in any situation. Number eight is considered immensely lucky in some areas of the world. However, this luck requires the same amount of hard work and dedication to accomplish the task at hand. Number eight is associated with the planet Saturn. When seeing this number as a message from your spirit guides, understand that you need to put in the work and ask not to slack and get up and reach the top of the mountain. It is also a message to tell you that if you put in the work required, you will accomplish it.

Number Nine

The number nine is the number of completion. It is the end of projects, relationships, or instances in one's life. It is not a number of death, but essentially a number of changes to come. Sometimes we need to let go of one thing to allow something else to move into our lives, and this is what the number nine symbolism as a message from your spirit guides conveys. If you are viewing this number frequently and are trying to understand the message behind what your spirit guides are showing you, try to look at the areas of your life that have perhaps reached their proverbial end. Maybe a relationship has become stale, and no matter what you do to bring the fires back, nothing changes. It is then wise to allow this relationship to go peacefully and lovingly.

The numbers from nine to 52 each hold a very definite meaning. Some share meanings with other numbers, especially when one reaches the forties. Regarding your path with your spirit guides, unless you have a substantial interest in numerology. The spirit guides will surely use less of this method and more of something you are naturally interested in. There is one certainty of the double digits, which is to alert you to your spirit guide's presence. For example, if you keep seeing 11:11 or 22:22 on the clock consecutively for a few days, make sure to sit down in meditation and ask your spirit guides for more clarity on their message. Sometimes it can mean that they want you to remember that you are not alone. Other times, it may be something a little more specific about a question that you have.

Inner Knowing

The intuition, the inner knowing that each person on this planet possesses, is the strongest gift that you have. Your intuition is your compass. It is one of the many built-in tools that you have to navigate your life. The world around us keeps us so busy that sometimes the messages from our own wisdom fall on our own deaf ears. You also need to have learned to trust yourself impeccably before trusting your intuition will ever happen. This bond with your own spirit is extremely important in getting to know your spirit guides and the messages they bring.

While reading this book, take your dominant hand and place it, palm first, on your solar plexus area, between the ribs and just below your chest. This area, known to the Hindu philosophies as the solar plexus Chakra, is where you can literally connect with your inner knowing and guidance. It is surmised that the umbilical cord that connects you with your spirit guide connects from this point (Laurie-Elle, 2019).

Some people feel more, others see or hear, and some people taste various things before certain events happen. The clair's, as they are known, fall into line with the different modes of manifestation from our inner knowing. There are six commonly agreed upon clair senses, and they are:

Clairvoyance - The ability to see visions. Those who have the gift of prophecy can see an occurrence before it takes place. Some have constant movie reels playing in their mind's eye and will see colors and symbols which will, over time, have specific meanings to them.

Clairgustance - Those with the gift of clairgustance will taste anything connected to the guide or to the circumstance at hand. For example, suppose they have been tasting licorice since they were a child each time they encountered their spirit guide. In that case, this taste then becomes associated with it. Similarly, the spirit guide will also speak to the person through their inherent gift, so perhaps the taste of garlic means something negative is about to happen. In contrast, a sweet taste in the mouth is a positive occurrence.

Clairaudience - while clairvoyance is known as the most prominent of the clair's, clairaudience would be second in line. Clairaudience is the gift of hearing messages directly. Apart from hearing audible voices, some people with this gift hear sounds instead of voice, or both. A sound will also be connected to a specific or series of events.

Clairalience - This clair is associated with smell. It is spoken of in the many books on exorcism that some negative spirits smell like sulfur. Someone with the gift or ability of clairalience will be able to associate certain smells with certain occurrences.

Clairsentience - Those with this ability or gift will feel actual sensations throughout their body. Their spirit guides will also alert them to specific messages by creating feelings like this. One very common clairsentient occurrence is feeling goose bumps when walking into a room and someone affirming the fact that peculiar phenomena have, in fact, taken place there.

Claircognizance - This clair is, in fact, called inner

knowing as well. While not many people believe that they have any of the claires, this one is the one clair sense that everyone shares. This clair is that knowledge that something is happening. It is a feeling that cannot be shaken, and regardless of what anyone else says, this knowledge cannot be argued with.

Regardless of how you connect with your spirit guides, the connection is a gift to you and your life. It can be referred to as a clair sense or by any other label. However, it can also be a combination of everything referred to above and more. There is no definite description of how you find your connection, and it is as unique as you are.

Books Falling off the Shelf

Apart from the myriad different ways your spirit guides can talk to you, there is the curious case of books falling off a shelf. Anything with written messages falls under this category. It is a definite sign from your spirit guide that they are nearby and that you need that message. It is important to hold the book between both hands with a book and ask whether your spirit guide wants you to read the entire book or simply a passage in the book. Using your inner knowing, you will be able to discern which of the two it is. If it is merely a passage, close your eyes, open the book, and place your finger anywhere on the page. Open your eyes and read what is written at the point where your finger is. Remember that the messages are always in line with your highest good, and sometimes they may not be what you want to hear but what you need to hear.

Sparks of Light

Sparks of light, orbs, or balls of light are all signs of spiritual connection. Seeing a spark of light in an area where there is no possible reason for the light to be present is a sign from your spirit guides that they are present. It is not as common to see orbs with the naked eye. However, they are viewed around animals, plants, and people just before it rains or on a bright day. It is more common to view any of these signs from your spirit guides through photographs. There is a big difference, though, between dirt and dust on the lens, movement of the camera and catching sight of your spirit guides. Many people have agreed that the sparks of light are, in fact, the spirit guides allowing you to see them in this dimension. There is absolutely nothing to be alarmed about, and they are always there to help and never harm. A negative entity will never show itself in pure light. So there is no need to feel anxious about such an encounter.

Free-Writing after Meditation

Meditation in itself can bring about many messages. However, the integration process between the conscious logical brain and that which we experience in meditation can be a completely different story altogether. For this reason, free-writing after any meditation session is extremely important to the understanding of symbols, patterns, and the overall messages.

Free-writing is as easy as keeping a journal or writing paper handy, with a working pen next to you before you go into meditation. Once you come out of meditation, take up the pen and begin writing everything that you experienced and everything that comes to mind while you are writing. There is no time frame set for this exercise, and you will know when you have come to full consciousness. You are analytically writing down what you remember. The inner critic is usually not present in this exercise straight out of meditation. Therefore there should be no judgment attached to everything that you scribble down.

Once the exercise is complete, leave the notes, take a break or a nap and return to the notes later. When looking at them, look at symbols and see the messages for what they are in a spiritual context. Try not to overanalyze and try more to use your intuition than your critical thinking.

THREE

Steps to Connect to Your Spirit Guides

HUMANITY AS A WHOLE IS A COMPLEX CREATION. WITH OUR current social structure, we are overwhelmed by the amount of sensory input and often lose sight of the incredible spiritual grace that surrounds us all the time. The mere fact that we are never alone can be a troubling thought to many people. This not being alone is not in the sense of the three-dimensional reality that we are experiencing. It is a shared experience of consciousness. It is not as though your spirit guide is watching you in the bathroom or following you around like a stalker. Your spirit guide is connected to you by the ether-body. The laws and physics of the spirit world work nothing like what our reality does.

Before you attempt to foster a healthy connection with your spirit guides and the positive changes in life that this will offer, you will need to develop trust. Trust in yourself and trust in letting go of fear. As Frank Herbert wrote in Dune, fear is undoubtedly the "mind-killer" (Herbert & Herbert, 2019). Not only does fear destroy the mind, but it tears away at the connection you have with your spirit guide. Simply letting go of the fear is not as easy as counting to three. It needs understanding behind it to see that there really is nothing to be afraid of in the first place.

The media has tarnished much of what we know about spiritual encounters. It has placed fear in many people's minds about possession and other atrocities, such as what if it is not your spirit guide and something sinister? This cannot be the case simply because you are the master of your life. Your spirit is the master of your body and mind, and absolutely nothing can take you over unless you give it permission. Secondly, intention is the master of all laws within spiritual work. If you couple your intention with your words and they work in unison, nothing can go wrong.

There are three fundamental laws about spiritual work within ancient practices: focus, will, and intention. When utilizing these three in harmony, then everything you do will have the desired outcome. When connecting with your spirit guides, these three fundamental laws need to be practiced in each of the exercises you practice to connect.

In the chapters that follow, you will be guided to practice specific methods in connecting with your spirit guides. You do not have to try all the techniques. It is advisable to read the book and then place your hand over your solar plexus and ask for loving guidance towards which method you will use to make a connection. If, and only if you have tried the technique for an entire month and nothing has come from the practice, try another method. It is not very likely that nothing will come from any process you are ushered towards trying. However, we sometimes need to try a few things before we unblock our own connections.

One more important note to explain is that your spirit guide is with you. There is no such instance where there is no spirit guide to be found; however, there is more than one spirit guide. Please remember when you utter words towards loving guidance. You are working in unison with your intention that your spirit guide is right there with you, helping you make this connection clearer in your mind. You are not making a connection per se. You are clearing away the active part of your mind and clarifying what is already there.

Patience is also required, and it is for that reason that a month per exercise is needed. A month may even be too little. In the Nordic spiritual paths, a rune practitioner was required to take up a single rune for six months to a year before they were allowed to move onto understanding and working with the next one. There are 24 of these runes in the Elder Futhark.

Spiritual work is not instantly gratifying, and then sometimes it is. It holds no hard and fast methods to anything, and it requires a flow within the practitioner. Spiritual work is also not fluffy in the sense that it will change you, it will dry your tears, but it will parent you and allow you to fix your life. In all these instances, you will be required to have the needed dedication and then listen to the received messages. Your spirit guides are with you for life, and nothing that you do will ever change that. Remember to foster a connection of love and compassion and steer away from controlling your spirit guide. Spirit is, after all, compassionate and loving, and it is built on your enlightenment. It must therefore be treated with the utmost love and respect.

Below is a guided meditation to connect you to one of your spirit guides. This meditation can be read by someone you trust to be part of the experience, or it can be read and recorded by you and then played back when you are ready.

To start, make yourself comfortable. Relaxing through this process is extremely important. You can lie down or be seated.

Close your eyes and begin at your toes, and end at your head. Tense every part of your body and then relax it.

Breathe in deeply when tensing each part of your body, and breathe out when you relax. When you are entirely at ease and feeling quite heavy.

Visualize yourself standing in a large open field. The grass is greener than you have ever seen grass to be. The breeze is moving the blades of grass slowly back and forth.

In the distance, there seems to be a dark cloud moving towards you. Perhaps it is a storm approaching? The center of this grass-covered area is a stone slab, it looks ancient, and you begin walking towards it.

Walking slowly, you notice that something is walking beside you. You look down, and to your left-hand side, there is an animal. This animal looks up at you with almost human qualities in its eyes.

Something is different about the animal. What is it? Are there any distinct markings on the animal? The animal urges you to look ahead, and you do so.

In front of you is an opening in the ancient slab of stone. It seems dark inside, but the animal reassures you that it is by your side.

Inside the entrance of the stone, the slab is a faint blue light. It allows you to see the staircase going down into the earth. You can smell the scent of soil, and it calms you.

The animal is still next to you but moves forward to walk ahead of you. It looks back and beckons to you to follow.

You begin the descent. One, two, three, four, five steps, six, seven, eight, nine, ten steps, each step is engraved with the most intricately designed symbols, and you wonder if you have seen them before?

Eleven, twelve, thirteen, fourteen, fifteen steps, now you catch sight of the source of the light. It is coming from the inside of a door that lies ahead. You step off the sixteenth step onto a landing, and still following your animal, you approach the door.

On the door is a sign; read it.

The door handle is large and brass colored, you turn the handle, and the door creaks open to expose an almost blinding blue light.

You shut your eyes for a moment until you can make sense of the landscape in front of you. There are tall majestic trees everywhere you look, and in front of you is a small pond.

The water reflects the painted sky. Look up at the sky; look at the paint that melts into itself over and over again.

You are nudged by your animal, and as you look down, you see that the animal has transformed into another sort of animal.

What animal is this? Is it an animal that you remember seeing? Or is it an animal from a book that you have read or a movie you watched?

The animal walks forward, and instinctively you follow.

Sitting at the edge of the pond is a humanoid being; as you approach, you see their face. A loving, beautiful face. This being looks up at you and speaks. You listen.

When the being is done speaking, they hand you a piece of paper, look at the paper, and write a sentence on the paper.

What does it say?

You fold the paper up and place it into your left pocket. The being holds you by the shoulders and turns you so that you face them.

It looks at you in your eyes, and you know this being. You feel comfortable, and you trust this experience.

The being explains to you that you will meet again soon. That they have always been with you, and whenever you are in need, that they will be right there to assist you.

The being places its right thumb on your third eye, right between your physical eyes, and rubs in a circular motion. At once, you feel your physical body again.

Keep your eyes closed. Breathe in deeply, and breathe out. When you feel ready, wiggle your toes, move your fingers and shift your body, opening your eyes, only when you feel prepared to do so.

As soon as you can write down everything that you experienced, as fast as possible without thinking about its logic.

There are thousands of guided meditations available online. It may take a while to find one that is right for you or one that works better than another. Nothing is frightening about using guided meditations. You can leave them at any time that if you feel, see or experience something you do not feel comfortable with.

FOUR

Start a Spirit Guide Journal

JOURNALING IS, WITHOUT A DOUBT, ONE OF THE BEST METHODS to integrate into your lifestyle regardless of the reason behind it. A spirit guide journal can also be used as a dream journal if you are inclined to have dreams. Everyone dreams, but not everyone remembers them. Our spirit guides love to bring messages through the dreamscape.

A spirit guide journal includes everything that you experience concerning spiritual messages and events. You can also begin to place partitions in the book that separate general spiritual encounters and those that seem to be particularly connected to a specific spirit guide. This way, you can begin to strengthen the bond between you and your spirit guide and understand their personality and method of bringing messages and guidance into your life.

A spirit guide journal is also a lovely gift to have around after many years. Like a family album, it shows the journey, growth, healing, and changes. The creation of a spirit guide journal does not have to be anything particularly lavish. It can be as simple as a plain notebook. Remember, as time goes on, there will be many of them, and some will be better adorned than others. Some will have more sketches in them than writing, and some will have torn-out pages and scratches from periods of frustration. Regardless of what the journals look like, the importance is in the journey. Knowing that this journey is between you and your spirit guide. These journals are the physical documentation of the path that you have taken from day one of your decision to finally make the connection.

Letter Writing

Letter writing should become a frequent occurrence in your life when attempting to establish understanding in your connection to your spirit guide. Letter writing involves you writing frequent letters to your spirit guide or to the spirit in general. These letters can be kept in a special box or folded into a holder.

In some traditions across the world, letters are written to spirit guides, and then once a month, they are bound with ribbon and thrown into a small fire with special herbs. The thought behind this is that they will travel up to the heavens, and the messages will be heard again. For other people, the simple process of writing the letter to your spirit guide allows you to strengthen the connection. Alert the spirit guide to what you are speaking about, almost like a sort of trance experience.

Writing in itself is incredibly healing. It is one of the preferred methods of releasing unwanted energies and laying down the foundation for solutions to come into play through connection while you are writing. Because of this frequent occurrence, it is wise to keep both the spirit guide journal open and the letter that you are writing so that when the solution or idea is placed into your mind, that you can write it down in your journal and will not have to get up and fetch something.

A letter to your spirit guide can be anything. It could be

you requesting assistance or simply letting out an emotional outburst and using your spirit guide's shoulder to cry on. It can also be a short note telling your spirit guides how much you love them and how grateful you are that they are in your life. There is no set size or set format that the letter needs to be in, but as a good practice, there should be a letter written once a week at least.

Expressing Gratitude

The exercise of expressing gratitude is one of the most important practices that you will undertake in this lifetime. Gratitude is not just words. It is a deep-set feeling inside your being that recognizes the magnitude of spirit and the enormous blessings in your life. Gratitude is not guilt-driven and should never be treated as such. It is a feeling that resides in the core of your being and, when felt, connects you with the entire spectrum of creation. Gratitude begets more of life to be grateful for, understanding that should not spur you on to be thankful because that is not gratitude.

Gratitude is a spiritual feeling. It comes from the soul, and when you experience it, you feel a connection with all life, both seen and unseen. This life that you live is so precious, these years that we have to experience everything and feel everything so deeply. It is not denied that spirit does have emotion, but it differs from our human experience. In spirit, there is said to be only love and compassion. It is said that there is no fear of loss, no sadness or grief, there is no longing or experience like humanity encounters.

The gratitude shown to your spirit guide or guides, or in the beginning, to the spirit in general, is a clear invitation for a more open connection to occur on a more frequent basis. Expressing your gratitude can and should happen twice a day. At least once you open your eyes, even before you climb out of your bed. The second time before you fall asleep. The times in between happen when you feel your spirit guide is close, or when you see something beautiful, or when an emotion envelops you. Your first action should be to express gratitude to the spirit.

List Making and Mind Mapping With Spirit

List-making and mind mapping are two ways to understand any subject better. Spiritual work is no different. Using either lists or mind maps; you can jot down all the experiences and see them in a condensed form, which allows you to understand them differently. Lists and mind maps are likened to a bird's eye view of anything. When we place all the experiences we have had in bullet form or in connected forms through mind maps, we see the entire picture with a new perspective.

Calling in Your Guides

There are many religiously affiliated ways and suggested ways by spiritual groups to call in your spirit guides. Many of them have some aspects in common, such as lighting a candle. It is said that the spirit world sees candle flames brightly and will come to your aid when you burn a candle. Another important factor is that of creating sacred space for yourself and the time spent in spirit.

Sacred space means a place where you are undisturbed and where you may feel spirit freely. For some people, this is outdoors. For others, it is a special place dedicated to prayer and meditation in spirit. It is important to remember to keep your spirit guide journal on hand during a session with your spirit guides as well as tissues. Just in case you become emotionally overwhelmed.

Calling your spirit guides can be done by simply seating yourself comfortably and stating your intention in your own words. Many people believe that they need someone else's words, and they need to get the words right, or the experience will not work. This is absolute nonsense, and in fact, completely opposite to the truth. When using your own words, they emanate from your own being, and nothing is more powerful than that. Remember that you hold all the wisdom you need within you, and because your spirit guide is already with you, all you need to do is ask.

Time Is Irrelevant

Time is a human construct. Time does not exist in the spiritual world. It is our own method of documentation and order inside the reality that we have found ourselves. It is apparent that time does not exist on the astral plane, and space is also quite different. If you look at the dreamscape, time does not exist at all, and some dreams can feel like years, whereas they have only lasted five minutes in real life.

Spirit guides work on their time, which is measured by the blueprint of your life. In other words, when you want something to happen today because there is some sort of urgency attached to it, understand that when it doesn't happen, it was not in line with your purpose for your life.

Sylvia Browne, a world-famous psychic, spoke extensively about how the spirit has its own time. Unlike how we veer off the chosen path, the spirit will not deviate ever, regardless of whatever you promise it. Our spirit guides are dedicated to us and our well-being. Our time is irrelevant to the greater plan, and they know it. Therefore our seemingly urgent requests will have no standing if they can see that there really is no impending doom. Sometimes we wish for something right now, thinking that it is the be-all and end-all, yet spirit sees that in ten years, it will be better suited as well as long-lasting. If that is the case, then so it shall be.

FIVE

Listen

WHEN WAS THE LAST TIME THAT YOU TRULY LISTENED TO spirits? When was the last time that you sat down and actually spent time in the stillness of the universal energy and simply experienced the magnificence of it all? When was the last time that you truly listened to anything or anyone?

Listening requires your full undivided attention for a set amount of time. It requires that you do not lose focus and that you absorb what is being listened to. If it is a person, then you are completely engrossed in what they are telling you. Suppose it is a piece of music that you are listening to. In that case, you are hearing every part of the melody, every twist, and turn of the notes, and you are doing nothing but listening. Suppose you are listening to two people talking at precisely the same time while looking at a video clip. In that case, you are not listening to any of the three. You are simply hearing them.

Scientists have found that multitasking is not all it is made out to be (American Psychological Association, 2006). We are never capable of multitasking. We are simply very poorly skilled or very adept in switching our focus between tasks. Our mind is only capable of focusing on a single task at any given time. Listening to spirits requires you to be undisturbed. It requires time, patience, and focus.

Prayer and Meditation

There is no practice more important than that of prayer. Meditation and prayer are similar in nature. However, prayer can be a form of meditation and vice versa. Their difference lies in that prayer is more of a giving approach from your side when not a form of meditation. In other words, you are speaking to spirits, you are making the connection, and you are sending your energy outwards. Meditation, on the other hand, is when we are in the space of receiving from spirits.

When we pray, there are usually two stages, the stage where we speak out loud or in our minds, and then the stage where we sit in silence with spirits. This second stage is where we find the solutions to the questions we have been asking or where we hear the voice of spirit. Our spirit guides sometimes have a tough time getting through to us through all the noise and constant chatter of the mind.

We are a talkative species. Whether it's talkative in the busyness of our mind or in the very recital of a thousand words, we do a lot of energetic expressions, and we do it all day long. Even in the dreamscape, we witness how busy our brains have been by viewing the replay of much of the excess thoughts and occurrences.

We need to find the stillness in our minds. We need to find the stillness in our souls and connect with that. Before you jump ahead and debate whether we can ever experience the state of no-mind, stop. There is no such thing as no mind. There will always be something, never nothing. However, there is quieting the monkey mind so that you may experience what your spirit guides are saying.

There are many methods of attaining stillness of mind enough to hear the voice of spirits. However, one easy way you can use across the board, even when you feel stressed, is simply observing thoughts. Close your eyes, take a proverbial step back, and watch your thoughts as they appear. When they appear, imagine placing them in a bubble and allow them to float away. Never fight a thought; never force a state of stillness, because this defeats the entire purpose. Once you have practiced this for a while, you will begin to find a space in between where there are ideas, thoughts, and messages that are outside of yourself. It is these that come from spirits.

The very act of meditation and prayer, or seating yourself in the spirit, is paramount to living your life through the guidance of universal energy. Regardless of the name that you call it, spirits exist. Humanity enjoys placing a label on everything and then arguing when no one will agree on their perception. Spirit is spirit, and it is not dependent on our perception of it. Prayer and meditation should be more important than brushing your teeth or building a career. Without guidance from spirits, we live empty lives driven by social constructs that we devised. We end up dying by the same social construct, with fear and emptiness.

SIX

Write With Your Spirit Guides
_____

PSYCHOGRAPHY, OR THE ART OF AUTOMATIC WRITING, IS A process where we let go of our control and decision-making and freely write. To obtain results like this, it is essential to remember the process mentioned in the previous chapter about the observation of thoughts. Once you can manage a quieted mind, you will be able to enter the correct frame of mind to perform automatic writing.

There is nothing to be feared through using this art form. Not only does the success in the process itself allow you to foster trust within yourself, but it is an excellent way to bring about deep healing from issues that you do not always realize are the problem.

Automatic writing is like daydreaming but with words, a pen, and paper. It is the same space in mind that you are using. Some people believe that automatic writing can only be done by those people who can channel. This is not the case. If you can practice stillness within your mind, then you can perform automatic writing.

Within this practice, there is no control on your part and absolutely no judgment. In other words, if you feel like you need to draw a circle around a specific word after writing it, then that is what is done. You are, in essence, following the unconscious messages that come out as urges within you and spur you on to write. The world enjoys making automatic writing quite a taboo subject, saying that a spiritual entity will take over your body and then write using your hand. This is impossible unless, of course, you are stepping out for a break and returning. Automatic writing does not need this or do this naturally. The act itself allows you to note that which your spirit guide wants you to know but which your mind is sometimes too busy to listen to.

When writing with your spirit guides, remember to set the intention, use a special space to do this, and light a candle. You must write the first thing that comes to mind, and this must happen at quite a pace and do not correct your spelling, grammar, or anything. Do not ask questions about what you are writing. Go with the flow and speed of the instance. You will know when you are done because your sense of needing to control will return. It helps considerably if you set the intention. Get ready, ask your spirit guide to be present, and then simply begin writing until the trance comes over you and then, of course, until you return to your normal conscious state.

There is absolutely nothing to be feared in this exercise or in any trance state. The peculiar aspect about any form of spirit work, meditation, and astral travel included is that no entity can ever possess you without your permission. No one can ever control you while you are in a trance either, because you will simply come back to a conscious state immediately. This is not the case if you have decided to use a hallucinogen to assist the process, which is never recommended. Spirit work does not need the use of external plants or medicines. You already have everything that you will ever need within you.

SEVEN

Ask for a Sign

TO BE HUMAN MEANS THAT WE WILL SEEK GUIDANCE, WHETHER in the realm of reality from friends, family members, or from something unseen in which we have a firm belief. Asking for a sign means that we are giving the universe, and our spirit guides the permission to intervene in our lives and provide us with proof that they are truly with us. Sometimes in our lives, all we really need is a sign that someone or something has our best interests at heart and that we are not alone in our endeavors.

When we ask the universe to intervene and show us some sort of sign they are with us, or even that the decision we are about to make is the right or wrong one, we have to be prepared to notice the sign. If we are not aware of our surroundings, we will not see the sign. It will have to be the size of a large boulder, dropping in front of us with a sign that reads:

"*This is the sign that you asked for.*
Kind regards,
Your Spirit Guide."

The likelihood of something like that happening is

extremely slim. The signs that we are given are usually subtle, although not always.

Signs are never as straightforward as we would like them to be, as spirit guides are not with us to spoon-feed us. We are meant to be making all the decisions with their guidance in mind, but the choice is ours to make at the end of the day. Spirit guides can and will never make the decisions for you. If the sign you ask for is simply for acknowledging their presence, make sure that you precisely request that. When requesting the spirit anything, be as specific as possible. The more specific you are, the less disappointed or confused you will be when the sign does appear.

Signs can be anything, from a feather to a billboard sign of a security company that says something along the lines of "… here to protect and guard your every move." However, the sign must be something that follows the request, coupled with a feeling that those words are for you. Signs can be tricky in that when we are looking for them, everything will appear as a sign, and in this comes the gift of discernment.

When we pray for a sign from the universe, we must have silence and patience within us. We must be aware of the feelings within our bodies as well as everything happening around us. It helps hugely when asking for a sign that you ask in a manner close to the prayer below.

Spirit Guide, please hear my prayer.
I need a sign that you are here with me.
Please let the sign be something that I will recognize and understand.
Please let me feel and see this sign, and have an inner knowing that this is indeed a sign from you.

When you have traversed the spiritual world enough, you will find something peculiar happens. You will see that everything in your life becomes a road sign. You will be guided in almost every waking moment. If you follow the detailed guidance, your life will be streamlined into such happiness that it may at times be overwhelming. In the beginning, though, signs are a careful art to understand, and sometimes you may get it wrong. Please remember to be patient and loving with yourself as you learn.

Each and everything in the universe holds the potential to be a sign. It all depends on our level of awareness and how many symbolic meanings we have come to integrate into our own cabinet of knowledge. Also, be very aware of the discussion earlier that stated that we only understand signs and symbols with our own meanings attached to them unless we have no meaning attached. We may seek out meaning from a trusted source.

Spirit guides are always happy to provide signs to you that they are with you. There is no short supply of creative ways in which they do it either. It can be a praying mantis landing on your computer screen in the early hours of the morning while you are asking for inspiration. A random hug from a child while walking down the street when asking for a sign that you are not alone. The importance is that you understand how signs work and that you trust in the process. Trust is critical for anything to work successfully.

EIGHT

Develop Daily, Weekly, or Monthly Spiritual Practices

WHEN YOU DECIDE ON MAKING CONTACT WITH YOUR SPIRIT guides, remember that everything does not come from spirits without you giving something from yourself. Time is one of the greatest gifts that you can sacrifice for spirits, time, and dedication. When we decide to take the leap forward and connect with spirits, we need to make sure that we are in it for the long run. Your spirit guide will never turn their back on you, but your lack of dedication may make you completely blind to their guidance.

It is therefore imperative to begin integrating certain routines into your lifestyle. Daily routines must include prayer and meditation or some sort of conversational aspect with the universe. Talking to spirits and your spirit guides are not talking to yourself at all. They listen to every word and every thought directed at them, and it is essential to remember that. When you are feeling down, simply having a chat with your spirit guide is one of the most mood-elevating experiences. Some people have reported actually feeling someone with them. What could be more consoling than knowing that your spirit guide is right there? Holding you and filling you with the energy of grace and love?

The second daily routine, which would be an excellent addition to prayer and meditation, would be to start your spirit journal, which we have discussed in Chapter Four. Weekly and monthly routines are just as important and build your connection with spirit. These routines can be anything from signing up and taking a yoga class. Joining a spiritual discussion group, taking part in martial arts, or finding a group of artists who create spirit art. It does not always have to include a group setting. A weekly or monthly routine can be a solitary visit to a holy place in your area or even a walk in a nearby nature reserve. Whatever routine you choose, remember to set the intention and then diarize it and not miss the date unless there is an emergency at hand. You would not like it if your spirit guides missed a date with you. Make sure not to do the same.

Reorganizing your life to be in line with your spirit will allow your spirit guides to know that you are serious. Do not be alarmed if you are unexpectedly showered with blessings from time to time. Spirits love to bless you. Your spirit guides will always bring your attention to everything that will bring you greater happiness and abundance.

Integration of Information

There are more varying beliefs in the world than you can imagine. Each person has added their own life experience and wisdom into their interpretation of the belief that they attribute to. Accordingly, there is no singular mind in any religion, spiritual path, or faith-based path. No two people can believe something in literally the same fashion because no two people are the same.

When learning about your spirit guide and the spiritual path that you find yourself on, you will have to come face to face with the opinions and variety of perceptions that lie outside of your own life. Firstly, there is no correct way of belief. There is no law that was not penned in by a human being and given to the entirety of humanity. Many prophets and people who have dedicated their existence have contributed profound material to the spiritual and religious fronts. However, each of their accounts are littered with their own human interpretation and level of awareness to accurately interpret what they are experiencing. It is for this reason that the spiritual path needs to be approached from an intuitive perspective.

Many people who belong to the same religion or spiritual path follow the same set of ideals and moralistic viewpoints; however, carrying them out is vastly different. Your own approach and ability to translate the symbols and messages of a spirit show you is dependent on your life. What experiences have you had? Who has been an integral part of your earlier years, and what sort of a person were they? What are your pastimes? Are you a sound of mind individual? Do you use hallucinogens? Do you have uncontrollable addictions? Do you get adequate sleep? The list of questions can fill a library. Yet, each one of them is important in understanding why you have chosen to resonate with specific experiences more than others.

For example, a woman who has experienced intense abuse from a fatherly figure will have a challenging time accepting that a male god is governing her. If she does accept this, she will not trust this entity very easily. It is a prominent finding that more women who have been subject to masculine abuse follow a Goddess-centered belief than a purely monotheistic male-dominated one (Griffin, 1995). We find spirit in the places where we feel peaceful or where our hearts, minds, and bodies feel cared for and nurtured for.

Spirit becomes a safe place, and this safe place will look like everything that your own life didn't. When you understand the psychology behind this, you will recognize the evidence within all scripture and spiritual teachings. When we read poetry, it is common to read about the poet, understand where this person brought their wisdom, and what may have influenced their brilliance. Similarly, when looking at any spiritual texts, understand the authors, understand the inspiration behind their teachings, and take from all teachings, only that which will make your spiritual path stronger.

Do not judge any path, including yours. You can and will never walk in another person's shoes, and nor would you ever want to. Your path belongs to you and their path to them. A spiritual path is a deeply personal journey that cannot be judged or fixed, or altered by anyone but the person on the journey. For example, suppose you were raised as a Catholic and find that on the spiritual journey, there are a thousand instances where you are breaking the laws of Catholicism and fear that you may be sinning. In that case, you are making a spiritual decision based on fear. This is not the spiritual way. God, Goddess, Spirit energy is one of love and compassion. There should never be any moment that spirits make you feel afraid or forced to do anything you do not want to do.

Never integrate a teaching into your being because a group of friends have found that it works, or because the marketing was incredible, and there are accounts of thousands of people who profess that this or that teaching saved them. Before learning a new teaching or deciding that any teaching must be integrated into your life, pray about it, ask spirit to guide you to feel if the instruction is correct for you.

Even the very connection with your spirit guide must feel right. If it doesn't feel right, then throw it out. Discard the whole process and move on with your life. You do not owe the time of day to anyone but yourself. Nothing in this world will give you the answers you are looking for except yourself. Within you are the answers to every question that you could ever ask. Within your being is the most powerful tool that you will ever own—your intuition.

Every single decision should be an act of love and compassion and confirmed by your intuition. You are not the world, you are part of it and can be a great agent of change, but you are not a blind follower on this path. This spiritual path is for those who wish to gain mastery of the self. Suppose you need to follow the crowd because they have learned through a specific teaching. In that case, the spiritual path you integrate into your being will only send you down the wrong path.

In Chapter 13, we discuss why you need to believe like a child and be a captain in the story. A captain of your own magnificent ship who knows, like the Hawaiian wayfinders, how to navigate the seas of life by using your intuition alone. Your spirit guide will assist you in every endeavor you choose to undertake. Still, you are the final decision maker. Integration into your life from teachers who never matched your moralistic beliefs will only allow you to lose valuable time. Your spirit guide will warn you time and time again. This information should become more trusted than any information ever documented by a human being.

Regardless of the path you encounter, there will always be a lesson to learn and something to gain, or else it would never have crossed your path. The subject of synchronicity is also essential to understand. Even if we do not integrate the spiritual path as a whole into our lives, we can incorporate a well-learned lesson if that is the case. Whatever the situation, if you feel that reading the tarot is not suitable because you cannot connect with it no matter what you try, try something else. The world around you is here to experience. It is here for you to learn from, like a massive obstacle course. If you live your entire life through judgment, fear, and preconceived perceptions, you will never live completely.

Allow the world to present to you the beauty that it has to offer. Through practicing a well-grounded, balanced spiritual path with your spirit guide, there is nothing that can stand in your way. When you allow a teaching or spiritual method to become part of your life, you begin the integration process, expect profound change. Every decision and integration that you bring into your existence will move your life around like chess pieces. There will be no change present, so make sure that the choices you make, the teachings you integrate are for your highest good and done with the loving energy of the universe. Before any decision, try to speak the following words before you come to a conclusion: "May the decision that I make now be in spiritual alignment with my highest good. May it be blessed by the light and love of the universe."

NINE

Pay Attention to the Guidance That You Receive

It is a peculiar notion that humanity would ask for a sign, ask for a miracle. When they receive precisely what they have asked for, they deny it and turn the other way instead. It doesn't sound like you would do something like that, but if you do have even the slightest trust issue; it will be a thousand times stronger when there is a crisis on hand. Perhaps asking for guidance on which ice cream flavor to choose would be an easy thing to follow. However, when faced with a life or death situation, would you still trust the opinion of your spirit guide? If the answer is no, you have much work to do to foster a greater strength within the relationship between you and your spirit guide.

When you invite spirits into your life, your spirit guides will be noticeably at your side without question. The more attention you give your spirit guide, the more you will be able to see, hear, feel and become aware of your spirit guide's hand within your life. When this happens, and when it grows stronger, nurturing this relationship only happens through trust. Trust the decisions, develop the relationship and become comfortable understanding that your spirit guide only has your best interests at heart.

Some people become fearful because their spirit guide did not assist them when they were suffering or when something seemingly awful happened to them. In the more significant explanation of the universe, understand that this reality is likened to a school with its many levels of learning. Even though you suffered, your spirit guide is truly with you to assist you in learning the lesson as fast as possible so that they can pull you from the wreckage and allow you to experience the happier side of life.

We need to look at why we were there or still find ourselves there through the bottom of the pit. What is keeping us in the darkness? If you ask such a question, ask your spirit guide for a sign to show you what is holding you down. This information is usually not pleasant and is, more often than not, one of the harder pills to swallow. It usually involves being faced with our own shadow sides. Look at what bad habits you have. If you are constantly poor, do you waste money, or do you have a gambling problem that you need to sort out? Do you perhaps have a person feeding off you, who you know needs to be let go, but you feel guilty? Guilt is never a choice, and if you experience any part of it in your life, you need to let it go right now. Guilt holds everyone involved in a proverbial prison and stops anyone from living their best lives.

Spirit guides will tell you what you need to know to help you find the best path for you. They will then expect you to acknowledge this information and follow it. When you do not follow it, they will not be angered at you but will be saddened by the continuous suffering you will endure while they cannot take it from you. They can only guide you out of the darkness.

TEN

Use a Divination Tool

DIVINATION TOOLS ARE ESPECIALLY WONDERFUL TOOLS TO integrate into your spirit guide connection path. They show you what is lying inside your subconscious mind and allow a sacred space for your spirit guide to work with you more directly. There are thousands of divination tools, some that have originated from ancient times and are still being used today. Others are being refined and redesigned to suit the modern era.

The art of using any sort of divination tool requires a focused mind, a clear set intention, and a time and space where you will be uninterrupted. Many divination practitioners make use of a sacred space that they have set up themselves. This space, as mentioned earlier, is entirely your design and must make you feel connected to spirit. It should always be kept clean and tidy, and the use of incense, essential oils, and candles allow for the vibration of the space to be lifted.

Divination tools are not an open connection to any spirit roaming around. The use of the Ouija board is not a recommended form of contact and nor is what is known as a "black mirror." The use of the Ouija board and the black mirror conjure up fear and unreasonable expectations in all who use them and this mere fact will cause the wrong sort of consequences to occur. It is wise to rather stay with user-friendly types of divination until you are entirely comfortable moving onto other forms.

It is also fantastic when your specific divination tool becomes part of your life. There is a flow of energy that you will experience after a while, or perhaps on the first try, and it is in this flow where the real magic happens. After a while, the connection becomes so concrete that you will be seeing the very symbolic items used in the divination tool in real life. They will carry with them meanings that will direct you.

Oracle Cards

Suppose you type "oracle cards" into Google. In that case, the results may overwhelm you, as there are as many oracle card decks as there are tarot. Oracle cards do not have a universal set system or structure. The entire oracle deck is based on the wisdom and guidance of the author. More often than not, the oracle deck will be accompanied by a booklet that will guide you through the in-depth meanings of the cards. It is also very common for authors of oracle decks to add in their own perception of the spiritual path. Perhaps give you a few meditations and reading spreads to work on. Each deck is unique. Some very prominent authors and leaders in the spiritual field will have more than one oracle deck available for you to choose from. It is also common for the author of an oracle deck and the tarot to have a spiritually inclined illustrator working on their project. Sometimes, like in the case of Alana Fairchild, she and Autumn Skye Morrison worked closely on an oracle deck entitled The Sacred Rebels. Autumn Skye has a history of creating breathtaking spiritual artworks. Coupled with her vision and the vision and years of spiritual teaching from Alana Fairchild, you have a magical union that will take you further into the core of your own spiritual path.

There are so many authors and illustrators that are worth mentioning in the oracle deck creations. However, the choice must be yours, and spending time searching for the deck that calls you is part of the joy of finding the oracle deck that works for you. If you are having trouble finding an oracle deck, try to search online for decks with a theme that is close to your heart. For example, if you love the fae, then look for an oracle deck with the fae.

Once you have found the deck that feels right, place your deck in your sacred space and open the cards. Hold them in your hands without looking through the cards. Hold the cards up to your heart and pray that your spirit guides will work through these cards to give you guidance for your life. It will always be delivered lovingly and compassionately that you will understand. Once you have done this, shuffle the cards and draw one card. Read the meaning in the booklet and making notes in your spirit guide journal of what the first card was. For the next week, it is recommended that you sleep with your oracle cards tucked under your pillow.

Tarot Cards

Tarot is vastly different from oracle decks. Both oracle decks and tarot are used for divination. Still, the tarot is different because it is a closed system based on prescribed rules and laws. Without venturing too far into the mysteries, there are two distinct versions of the tarot that originated, apart from the tarot that we see to have developed in Italy around the fifteenth century. Many tarot readers and diviners have never used these original tarot decks because they are not found without error in the print or not found in print.

To venture into these original decks and why the truths

were hidden so well in a new system where it was watered down but still kept with a systematic approach will take many years of study. The tarot found today has many variations as well. The variations lie within the interpretation of the creators, both author, and illustrator. The tarot has a generally accepted number of 78 cards split into the major arcana and the minor arcana. The major arcana consists of 22 cards, each representing an archetypal figure or message. The minor arcana consists of 56 cards, split into four suits. These suits correspond with the modern playing card suits of diamonds, clubs, spades, and hearts. In fact, if you are an adept tarot reader, you will be able to divine with playing cards alone.

It is also possible to read with only the major arcana if you so wish, as these cards tell a complete tale of the soul, body, and mind. The minor arcana become complimentary cards in a reading and lend more detailed information to the reading as a whole. Tarot requires dedication and time that is only found in the study. Still, when you have mastered the art of reading tarot, you will have also mastered the art of the psychological and magical journey of the self. When choosing a tarot deck, it is wise to begin with a starter tarot deck. A deck that sticks to the Kabbalistic, planetary, numerological, and elemental symbolism. Many of the newer decks are extremely beautiful. They will pull you in, but tarot needs the study to avoid frustration and misinterpretation, unlike the oracle.

In the end, it is only another divination system. However, tarot does more than provide simple day-to-day divination. It opens an entirely new world of meaning. It lifts the veil to many things that are sometimes not needed on an early journey into what the Celts referred to as the otherworld. Below is a quick guide to the meanings of the cards of the major arcana. As per the Rider Waite interpretation, please note that each card also has a corresponding number that connects to numerological symbolism.

The Fool - 0 - Taking the leap of faith into the unknown. Leaving the areas of comfort behind. Trusting in spirit.

The Magician - 1 - Bringing spiritual energy into the process of manifestation. Understanding your own power in life. Having everything that you need to achieve the results that you desire.

The High Priestess - 2 - The process of inner knowing needs to be exercised. There is also something hidden from view. You have the knowledge that you need within you.

The Empress - 3 - Fertility, motherhood, and all aspects of the divine feminine mother. Feminine dominance.

The Emperor - 4 - The father, systematic structural outlook. Planning. All aspects of the divine masculine are present.

The Hierophant - 5 - Spirit guide or physical guide within a spiritual or religious setting. Learning is taking place. Beware of dogma.

The Lovers - 6 - When two become one. The meandering path. Choice is at hand. Choose wisely, choose from the balance of heart and mind.

The Chariot - 7 - Movement, forward motion. Willpower, balance is prevalent here.

Strength - 8 - Facing the beast within, taming the inner turmoil. Calm control needs to be exercised. Trust in the process.

The Hermit - 9 - Completion stages. Introspection. Inner knowing and wisdom is a time of information that needs to be integrated into the self.

The Wheel of Fortune - 10 - The hand of fate always turns. A prosperous outcome. There is a chance of good fortune present.

Justice - 11 - Legalities may be present—karmic law in action.

The Hanged Man - 12 - Stuck in the mud. Ask for guidance on how to bring the energy of the Chariot into the situation.

Death - 13 - Complete transformation. The end of a cycle has come into play. Accept the transformation and do not fight it.

Temperance - 14 - Balance is paramount. Finding the correct synergy in the situation.

The Devil - 15 - Addictions need to be addressed. Materialism is at play and needs to find balance with spiritual beliefs.

The Tower - 16 - Change through the process of destruction.

The Star - 17 - Renewed spiritual love and compassion.

The Moon - 18 - Mental problems. Anxious attitudes. Depression. Illusions.

The Sun - 19 - Masculinity. Strength. Vigor. Intense happiness.

Judgment - 20 - Forgiveness is for the self and outside influences. Completion to a stage is almost at hand.

The World - 21 - Completion. Attainment of a goal. Final stage (Esselmont, 2018).

Each card, both in the major arcana and in the minor arcana, has a corresponding reversed meaning. When a card is reversed, it is drawn upside down, and the meaning changes. This is entirely up to you and your personal style. There are enough cards within the deck to get your message across, and some practitioners prefer to keep the deck upright. Others will flip handfuls of cards multiple times in the shuffling process to insert reversed cards into the deck. Most decks will come with descriptions of each card's meaning, reversed and upright.

Runes

There are many forms of runes across the globe. One of the better-known runes is the runic divination method of the ancient Norse people. Even though this divination system has now branched into many different variations, its origin lies within an ancient magical system called the Elder Futhark. The Elder Futhark is a set of 24 runes, without the modern-day addition of a blank rune. When redrawn in red as a closed circle, starting with Fehu and ending with Dagaz, it becomes a powerful protection symbol in itself.

The Elder Futhark was used as a magical connection to those who dwelled in the nine worlds contained in the world tree known as Yggdrasil and the world around the people who used them. The lore attached to the original form of the runes will take a lifetime of dedication and study to understand everything. Even though modern advice places no emphasis on the broader journeys of the runes, it must be noted that this is not an undertaking for the faint at heart.

Runes are witnessed in many corners of the media today. Apart from being a divination system, they are initially a magical system filled with incredible power connected to the subconscious mind. Suppose you choose to venture into a deep understanding of the spirit realms and wish to do more than simply connect with your spirit guide or guides. In that case, no system on this planet holds more lore and magical connection coupled with mundane understanding than the Elder Futhark.

The Nordic path of today is filled with a large number of opinionated groups, and it is best to remain neutral in the approach to your study of this divination system. The spiritual attachment connected with the runes is a lively one and will alter your life and shift it into a gear that is best suited to your own blueprint of purpose.

Whether you choose to learn mediumship, scrying, dowsing, cartomancy, or begin reading tea leaves or coffee grounds, your journey will be a rich one if you stick with the divination method until you, the student, does indeed become the master.

There is never any reason to leave a particular field of study, especially if you have made the dedication to spirit. Every path you take will yield results, not because the divination method is powerful but because you are opening yourself up to the possibility of so much more in the universe.

ELEVEN

Stay in the Energy of Gratitude

You have so much power within you, one of the great gifts you have right this second is gratitude. Gratitude is spoken about a lot, with just cause. Gratitude heals your entire life. This unseen force that cannot be held, or boxed, moves through your body like a wave of grace. It is ironic then that the word grateful comes from the Latin word gratia, which may also mean grace.

Gratitude is an overwhelming power that, when experienced, seems to stop time itself. It immediately places you in that very moment and then seems to expand outwards. When we find gratitude towards anything in our lives for an endless amount of time, we will find gratitude for a thousand more things. Simply because gratitude itself permeates throughout the universe.

Gratitude has been studied extensively by many leading physicians, psychologists, and even the military. It has been concentrated on even more in the present day and age because the astounding effects cannot be ignored. Not only does gratitude wake up the mind and release all your happy chemicals in your brain, but it promotes healing and wellbeing on such an incredible level that it changes people's entire lives.

Gratitude is contained in many papers concerning the subject of positive psychology, which, according to Christopher Peterson, is "the scientific study of what makes life most worth living" (2008). Gratitude is the beginning of all happiness, it is the most straightforward starting point, and it comes from within you. If you are thinking that there is nothing to be grateful for, then you are sorely mistaken. Look around you, from the very breath in your body to the blood running through your veins. To the life you have, the sunshine outside, and the world around you. If you can be grateful for nothing else, be grateful for the conscious life that you are living. Begin with something small in your life. Gratitude is shown every day will bring you greater happiness and a more positive state of mind, less illness, and more stuff to be grateful for (Harvard Health Publishing, 2011).

Begin your gratitude with a thought, an observation into your life. Look only for one thing you are grateful for, and then write that down in a book dedicated only to gratitude. Place the book in a place where you find yourself sitting every morning or evening, and then write that one thing in your book each time you sit there for a week. In the second week, add another thing that you are genuinely grateful for, and so on. Until you can only write what you were grateful for that day, and it will become an entire page. When you have completed the journey of the gratitude journal, you can simply wake up, stretch and breathe in the magnificence of the universe and of spirit and find gratitude within that experience.

The busyness of your life does not only make you miss much of what spirit is teaching you and trying to communicate to you, but it makes you miss the small things in your life that you actually have so much gratitude for. In Tai Chi, for example, you must relax because otherwise, you will hurt yourself in some of the moves. Similarly, you need to relax, breathe in the universal energy, and actually feel gratitude before you can truly show it.

When dealing with your spirit guide, remember to show gratitude for each and every encounter and really feel it within you. This will strengthen the bond and allow your spirit guide to feeling welcome and needed in your life. The more gratitude you show towards the experience, the more guidance and assistance from the spirit will occur.

Your Gratitude Keeps Your Relationships Strong

Gratitude is not just a word. It is a feeling. It is not enough to provide lip service to your partner or to your family, friends, and community members, because we do not only communicate physically. Humanity communicates through an unseen network of energy that we have only just begun exploring. There are other dimensions and a more meaningful existence inside our own minds, let alone the universe outside ourselves. Physicist and Author Dr. Michio Kaku speak extensively about the physics behind the greater dimensions than ours and those potentially much smaller. He also explains in great depth how everything is energy.

A force as powerful as gratitude brings any relationship with you into such incredible harmony that it becomes almost unbreakable. The feeling is what makes gratitude, though, and the feeling communicates and strengthens this bond between two or more people. When you say thank you, mean it. If someone in your life irritates you or brings you to anger, look within. Nothing in this life is one-sided. Everything, including you, has two sides, two polar opposites living as a single being. For this reason, feeling irritated, angered, or experiencing any other negative emotion means that there is also something within you that needs to change.

Take, for example, a parent who is negative all the time. In this instance, you are attempting to remedy your life and learn about meeting your spirit guides and following your own heart.

Yet, this parent is trying to place stops in every decision that you have on the path. The way to deal with this is to see that perhaps the parent has had an intense negative experience. Or has been told bad things about the spiritual path and contacting spirit guides and is trying to protect you. On your side, perhaps you are opening your parents' eyes too fast. Maybe their life is not ready for what you are experiencing, and in an instant such as this one, your own spiritual path must be kept to yourself.

Never lie to please people. Simply find an alternative route to bring peace and harmony to yourself and to all who are involved. Remember that each and every relationship that you have is with a whole person just like you. Everyone has fear, emotional ups and downs, and their own perceptions of this reality. Your path is never the same as anyone else, not even that of your spouse or of your children.

If you want the relationship in your life, nurture it. Ask yourself, before any gratitude, why this person is in your life, and why you feel the need to keep them in your life? Then look for why you are grateful that they are in your life, write this down. Keep it in your heart and in your mind when you deal with this person and allow yourself to feel gratitude when you are speaking or interacting with them. When you do this, their seemingly irritating behavior seems to slip away.

There is a curious case that should be mentioned. However, names have been changed for the privacy of the people involved. A mother and her son had been living in the same home, and she had never wanted the child, but to appease her own parents, she kept the child around. At the age of eighteen, this child had had no schooling and was grossly overweight. He had absolutely no social skills except the discussions that he kept with friends over the internet and games with other gamers. His entire life revolved around the lives of the people worldwide on the server he was part of. Deep inside, this child knew and felt no gratitude, no love, and only apologized continuously for him being around.

A case such as the one above is not even the most serious accounts; there are others where spouses are only in relationships for financial reasons. Children are observed and cared for because of the public image. Still, there is an emptiness of gratitude for many connections worldwide. If there is no gratitude to be found, either end the relationship and trust the universe to walk alongside the spirit guides and find liberty and your true purpose or find gratitude and find meaning in the relationship at hand. There is no middle ground. There is no reason why you should be holding onto something which is forced or which is pretended. Not only is it destructive to your own health and wellbeing, but it is cruel and heartless towards another person.

That being said, despite the incredible myriad nuances that make up every relationship, remember that gratitude is the core of all other feelings that permeate through the connection. This is paramount in the relationship with you and your spirit guide as well. Gratitude brings healing. It makes room for love and compassion. It calms the soul, nurtures the spirit, and feeds life towards greater happiness. Without gratitude, there is only an empty, materialistic forward movement towards a pointless death. If it is healthy relationships that you are looking for, then find everything to be grateful for and bask in its grace and glory.

TWELVE

Release the Outcome and Trust in a Better Plan than Your Own

Neuroscientist Beau Lotto, Author of Deviate: The Science of Seeing Differently has studied the science behind perception extensively, and in his book, he welcomes the world to see differently. The science is remarkable, the idea, simple and right in front of your eyes. The consequences of changing perception are numerous and, as of yet, unquantifiable. However, the data is growing, and the explanations on a simple change in how we perceive the world are astonishing in the least.

The pre-Columbian Mesoamerican culture, known as the Toltecs, held a pearl of wisdom about the very art of perception. In this wisdom, they speak of an axis of perception that we all have. It is perhaps likened to a horse with blinders on, how we travel through our lives. A single perception and a single mode of living. It is only through intense trauma or a miraculous act from the hand of fate that changes this perception and removes the proverbial blinders. The Toltecs advise those who are to conquer the world they live in to ensure that their axis of perception is fluid. In other words, it must be able to move according to the situation that they are found in. You must learn to perceive from the other person or people's viewpoint and your own, and the consequences involved must also be perceived.

This is not an easy thing to accomplish at all. Changing your perception and undoing a lifetime of socialization is quite a task. It is imperative, though, and on the path of understanding spirit and finding your spirit guide, the information that you gain will alter your perception in any case. To make it fluid, though, you will need to let go of what you believe to be factual and concrete.

Nothing in the world that we live in is concrete. Not even concrete is concrete, as it is made up of atoms with dancing electrons. Therefore, the entire universe is unequivocally moving all the time. Suppose the universe is moving, dancing, and changing. Why are most humans so adamant about staying fixed in their viewpoint, frozen in time with their own ideas of why their lives are the way they are?

You do not have all the answers. However, you do have access to all the answers. All you have to do is "let go and let Spirit take the wheel and drive" (Schutte, 2009). Changing your perception is one thing. Allowing spirits enough trust to make the decisions is an entirely different ball game altogether. These are the two aspects of spirit communication that are imperative. In fact, if you want to master anything that was ever written about abundance thinking and self-empowerment, then gratitude, change of perception, and trust in spirit is the only recipe that works.

It is not simple to change your perception overnight. Still, it is simple enough to trust in your spirit guide and in spirit as a whole and allow the blueprint of your life's purpose to be instituted into your life now. We are minute specs within a more remarkable design that we have not even begun to understand. When we realize this fragility of our own nature, we know that the spiritual aid given to us is for a reason. To utilize it within our lives can only add positive results.

Spirits see the bird's eye view of all life in a single moment.

Your spirit guide is appointed to guide you onto the path of your purpose. It ensures that you are accompanied and nurtured throughout your journey. Letting go into the hands of your spirit guide does not remove your control over your life. The choices are always in your hands, you are always the captain of your ship, and nothing can change that. It's called free will.

Guidance is necessary on this path, a necessity that should not be refused because, with it, your life will change dramatically almost overnight. Suppose you heed the call of your spirit guide and truly listen and follow all the wisdom that will come from such a relationship. In that case, the happiness and the joy that you have been longing for will be yours. It is a life-altering experience that the words of any language fall short of explaining. It is an experience that must be felt by you. You must be exposed to its miraculous nature if you wish to exercise the change that is knocking at your door right now.

THIRTEEN

Be More Childlike

IN THE TEACHINGS OF JESUS CHRIST OF NAZARETH, IT IS documented by the apostles Luke and Matthew that Jesus himself spoke about how to be like a child, or to have faith like a child is the only manner in which you will enter what the Christian faith refers to as the Kingdom of God.

Children are impressionable, naive, playful, trusting, and imaginative. A child can imagine an entire universe between two chairs, a duvet, and a flashlight. The younger the child, the less reason the child has to remain angry at anything for longer than a few minutes. In fact, one of the most delightful experiences is to witness how easily a child forgives and carries on with their day. They hold such potential, such innocence, such lack of adult emotional baggage and chaos. Adults often refer to children as chaotic and disturbing to their own peace. Still, they spend an afternoon playing like a child again, and your faith in the magic of the world will be renewed.

Our inner child archetype needs a large amount of attention, love, and care. We forget that we were all children once, and to a large extent, we still are. When the doors are closed to the outside world, we are vastly different from when we are faced with society. This person that emerges when we are alone is our inner child waiting to burst out and dance down the passage with the mop in hand. Singing all the false notes at the top of our voices, sliding on our white socks, and reenacting a scene from Star Wars with a slice of melting cheesy pizza in our hands. When did life get so serious? When was the moment we actually buckled down and had to conform to the social structure? It was the exact moment that you forgot how to recognize the voice of spirits. And the precise moment when you forgot to play hide and seek with your spirit guide in the garden.

Every child is unique, and even though not all children want to go dancing with the mop down the passage, we all hold a part of that childlike nature within us. It's more prominent than you understand. It contains the key to understanding the universe and experiencing the happiness that you so long for. To believe like a child means that you can see the universe in its entire splendor again. It means that you can look through the holes of the trampoline netting. Utterly exhausted from jumping, and see the sun rays fall on the blades of grass below, dancing with the shadows from the trees blowing in the wind. You can imagine an entire universe existing down there.

Being childlike is not being childish, and this is where being an adult becomes important. We need to hold onto the childlike innocence, purity, wonder, and trusting nature of our inner child. Still, we must also allow the immaturity to fall away. This immaturity can cost us our livelihood in the social structure. It is imperative to find a healthy balance between being an adult and making time to be our childlike selves again.

Adulthood also brings with it experience. Experience brings with it ten-foot walls with spikes and baggage packed until kingdom come. It teaches us never to trust anyone, remain isolated and work until our fingers have been ground down to the bone. It teaches us that playing with cards and imagining beautiful futures is a complete waste of time. It teaches us that we need to climb over our fellow humans and keep the biggest toys for ourselves. It teaches us all the wrong things.

In the game of life, we swamp ourselves with bills and responsibilities, and we tell our inner child to keep quiet, sit still, and go and find a dark, quiet space to busy themselves in. We carry on and become confused as to why we feel so darn unhappy with life. It is simply because our inner child has been sent away, and no child likes that. A part of ourselves is missing. Nothing can function adequately if a large amount of itself is not working correctly.

Make time to nurture the inner child, find time to be childlike again. If you make space for these experiences, you will gain your childlike belief again, and you will have restored your perception of the world. This is the path to a fluid axis of perception. This is the strength that you have been seeking. This is the part of you that will open your eyes to see your spirit guide because it is the child within that holds the key to spirit communication.

FOURTEEN

Ask Your Spirit Guides for Their Names If You Feel Called To Do So

THE CONNECTION BETWEEN YOU AND YOUR SPIRIT GUIDES WILL strengthen over time. Once again, you need to remember that only you learn to see them and improve your bond with them. The spirit has always been with you, so this is a case of recognizing and reaffirming the trust from your side. Your spirit guide, or guides, will be with you every step of the way.

When asking your spirit guides anything, please understand that it may take some time before answers become as straightforward as you expect them to be at the beginning. A lot of patience is required, and be gentle with the process. Do not force anything. That only creates negative energy. Approach everything in the moment and with a relaxed, flowing attitude. Regardless of the questions that you have for your spirit guide, they will provide answers where they are able. Otherwise, they will simply direct you to find the answer yourself if that is what is necessary on your path.

Communication will come in many forms. For this reason, employing a divination method, as discussed in Chapter 10, is wise in the beginning. Another tool works if you intend to ask for your spirit guide's name or a name of a person, place, or thing. You could use automatic writing, but such an undertaking takes practice and greater levels of trust than the use of loose letters.

Acquire for yourself a material pouch. It does not have to be velvet. In fact, it can even be a plastic bag if you have nothing else. Inside this pouch, place three sets of the letters of the alphabet. If you have decided to use the runes as your choice of divination, the runes themselves have been equated to letters. They can therefore be used for this exercise as well. The letters themselves can be made of wood, paper, plastic, or any other handy material. The fridge magnet letters designed for children can also be used.

Once you have your bag of letters or runes ready, light a candle, seat yourself in your sacred space, and greet your spirit guide. Remember the childlike discussion, if you start to feel that this exercise is stupid or worthless, get up and go and do something else, or quieting the mind and return to your meditation. Once you feel ready, place the bag in front of you, ask your spirit guide to use the channel of your intuition to guide you to pick out the letters of their name. Explain why you would like to know their name, and when you are ready, place your hand in the bag and pick out the letters one by one. Do this exercise with your eyes closed. Do not do it with haste and feel your way into choosing the letters, do not think about it. The brain is useless in such an exercise. It is the intuitive channels you are working with.

When you pull each letter from the bag, place it side by side, in order in front of you on the floor, or even a table, whatever is more comfortable for you. When you feel that you have picked out all the letters, open your eyes and read the name out loud. Greet your spirit guide with this name, and show gratitude for the experience. If the letters make no known sense, remember that they could be from a language you do not speak. You can find a nickname for a name that you cannot pronounce and ask your spirit guide if suitable. Use your divination tool to receive an answer.

Remember to write the name of your spirit guide down in your spirit guide journal. You can even make art from the name, place it on your wall in your sacred space, or create a page in the spirit guide journal to honor your spirit guide. If you feel compelled to look up the name and do research on your spirit guide, then do that, but if you find nothing, remember that does not mean that your spirit guide does not exist. It simply means that maybe their human life was not deemed necessary enough to document or that they have never had human life to begin with. Also, only ask the name of your spirit guide to strengthen the connection, not for validation, as this will harm the relationship between the two of you. The mere decision only stems from distrust in your own spiritual experience.

FIFTEEN

Trust in Your Own Psychic Ability

TRUST IS DEFINED IN MANY DIFFERENT WAYS; HOWEVER, ONE OF the more straightforward definitions is "a belief in the reliability, truth or ability of someone or something," (Merriam-Webster, 2019). Looking at this definition, trusting yourself and your own visions means that you believe that what you are experiencing is reliable and truthful. It also means that you believe that you can have psychic experiences.

Psychic experiences are defined as "lying outside of the sphere of physical science or knowledge," (Merriam-Webster, n.d.). This means that any feeling that you have ever had, any hunch, any use of your intuition has been a psychic experience. Psychic does not only mean that you can perceive the illnesses in people's bodies like medical intuitive Caroline Myss can. Or that you can speak to the dead as psychic Sylvia Browne did. Psychic means that any moment that you have ever arrived at a conclusion or found an idea that did not use factual evidence that you have had a psychic experience.

When we break down the psychic abilities to their simplest form, they do not seem so daunting or frightening. If everything in the universe is energy, then how can we deny such experiences? In the greater scheme of the universal understanding that we have come to thus far in our evolution, every human seems to have had some sort of psychic experience in their lives throughout history. Dreaming of solutions to problems that belong to people who live far away that you have never met, such as Edgar Cayce, seems to be something that happens only to other people. It also appears that sometimes the media takes the ball and runs with it because these sorts of phenomena sell. However, psychic experiences are really understood by mothers, who can feel their children are in danger, or they receive a feeling that their child needs them. When they reach out, the child was, in fact, wishing that they would phone.

You belong to a network of energy. Each and every person on Earth is connected somehow. The science on this has not yet caught up. Still, we have incredible volumes of data from cultural experiences across the globe. We also have a mass awakening in the world, where speaking about such topics is no longer something that needs to be hidden. This means that everyone who is having a conscious psychic experience for the first time can now reach out and buy a book. Make an appointment with an appropriate specialist in the field they are asking after, or find a mentor.

It is much easier to look at someone who has been in the awakened state for many years and have awe in your perception of them and their abilities. However, those same abilities that you are awe-struck by are usually the same abilities that you possess. We often marvel at something outside of ourselves because we have the same talent. Perhaps it is latent for the moment. Still, it's something that is in our grasp.

If you are not familiar with your psychic abilities and have had some sort of psychic experience, and are curious to find out more, simply ask aloud. Begin reading books on the topic, watch seminars on TEDx, go to meetings with other people who are waking up to their abilities, and share experiences. There are an entire host of exercises to build your psychic ability to be practiced. Each guide on this path will have their own version of these practices, and some of them will work wonders for you, and others will not.

The core aspect that must be learned before you venture into any group or find a mentor is self-trust. No exercise or mentor, or book will ever be able to make you trust yourself. Without trust in the self or knowledge of the self, anything you do will be met with doubt, fear, and apprehension, therefore giving you a halfhearted approach. To love someone outside of yourself, you need to love yourself. To trust anything outside of yourself, you need to trust yourself first.

You are your own worst enemy and your own best friend. Always remember that. If you do have a tough time trusting your own intuition and second-guessing everything that happens or brushing it off as not necessary, or a stroke of luck or madness, then try the following affirmations in their order, every morning when you wake up and every night before you go to sleep.

Stand in front of the mirror, or hold up a handheld mirror and look yourself in the eyes as though you were telling this to a dear friend who needed to understand a truth that you knew. Now say the following affirmations only once, but seriously, and with great empathy: "You are loved. You are enough. You are dignified. You are beautiful. You are awake. You are genuine. You are graceful. You are spirit. You are worthy. You are divine. You are perfect."

After one month of doing this set of affirmations every single morning and every single evening before bed, you will begin to see positive changes in your life. You will slowly start to trust your own nature, your own abilities, and your own mastery within your own life much easier than before.

SIXTEEN

How to Ground Yourself after Connecting With Your Spirit Guides

Before we jump into why and how you should ground yourself after you have completed any session in spiritual work or with your spirit guides, we must jump into what is generally known as grounding. Earthing, or grounding, is the act of standing on the bare earth and balancing your own energy through connecting with the energy of the Earth. However, the act of removing any excess charge from any object is also called grounding.

Grounding is not only imperative after any session with your spirit guide. It is essential every day of your life. When we are not grounded, we are not entirely in our conscious waking state. We are roaming the dimensions of thought in spiritual terms, or half in, half out of our bodies. The well-known saying that describes someone who is ungrounded is "that person seems to have their head in the clouds." This could not be closer to the truth. When you are not matching the frequency of the earth, you are not here. There are so many partitions to who we are, more than we have an awareness of on this physical plane. However, we need to live in this reality, and so we need to ground ourselves.

Almost all ancient cultures have tales of grounding by

connecting with Mother Earth. The benefits of grounding that science is beginning to find slows down the aging process, speeds up healing, and reduces pain (Chevalier, 2012). Sleep and the natural circadian rhythm are also returned to normal. It is important to remain grounded and stay connected to the earth's frequency. When you are leaving this state of consciousness and receiving outside information, you will not be grounded when astral traveling or doing meditations. Still, if you have practiced grounding, you will return to this state when you have completed your session.

Now that you have an idea on grounding, it is necessary to explain what happens when we connect with our spirit guides. Enter into a spiritual plane, leave our bodies, or pray fervently. Our consciousness remains in this vehicle while we are grounded and present in this reality. However, our consciousness can traverse a thousand worlds in a millisecond here on earth when any spiritual work is done. A conversation with people whom we meet happens on two spheres. There is the apparent physical sphere that takes place here. Then there is the unconscious sphere where information is being picked up all the time. Some people, who are aware of their psychic abilities, will be mindful of both the physical experience and the spiritual experience taking place. In this connection, you can pick up whether a person is being truthful. Whether they have a hidden agenda or even whether they are hiding an emotion that needs to be addressed. This is especially useful to intuitive therapists.

When we are not grounded, we are constantly receiving information about everything around us. This leads to exhaustion, as well as an inability to feel the present moment completely. A session with your spirit guide can completely drain you if you are not adept at exchanging information on a psychic level. If you do feel drained of energy at any time or spiritual work, it is essential to ground. There are many ways to ground yourself, including using Earthing products patented as methods of treating inflammation and autoimmune diseases. The products which can be purchased range from sleep kits to house mats and so forth. If you have access to a natural setting, grass, or beach sand, the natural way would be best. It is a surefire sign of how incredibly built up our modern lives have become. So many people have no access to space where there is a natural setting. It is for people like this that the Earthing products are for.

Grounding by walking outside and placing as much surface area of your body close to the Earth's surface is the most beneficial way to ground yourself. Your bare feet on the ground are just as helpful, but lying down on the ground works faster. In some ancient and modern-day rituals, it is essential to raise energy through music and dance and then send this energy with an intention out into the universe. After this is complete, grounding occurs by standing barefoot on the ground as well as placing the palms of your hands flat on the Earth's surface. Practitioners will do this until they can feel that they are present in the moment and utterly conscious within their own bodies again.

Grounding can also be obtained by wearing black, brown or red, or keeping grounding crystals on your person. Some grounding crystals are onyx, obsidian, hematite, and black tourmaline. Another way is to surround yourself with grounding scents. This is done by using essential oils in burners or humidifiers, burning the plant itself on a coal in a seashell, or using specific incense. Some scents will allow you to leave your physical body. Others will ground you. One last method that works wonders after a session with your spirit guide or a meditation session is to keep a bowl of cooked potatoes handy for after the session. Snack on potatoes or radishes, and you will feel more grounded. Of course, the most beneficial method is to be physically in touch with Mother Earth. Still, if that is not possible, then any of the methods as mentioned earlier will work.

SEVENTEEN

Spiritual Shielding and Defense

INTEREST IN THE SPIRITUAL REALMS AND EVERYTHING IN between, comes with curiosity. Even though the cat has been rumored to have nine lives (symbolic), curiosity did kill the cat at the turn of each cycle. Everything that you do within your life needs balance. You need a healthy dose of sleep, nutrition, happiness, sadness, excitement, and care. There are so many parts of you that you will begin to know when you step on the path of spiritual enlightenment. It will be challenging to stick to a single interest until it has been completed or mastered.

During the process of connecting with your spirit guide, there are definitely a few warnings that come with the practice. Before we dive headfirst into the warnings, think for a second about the nature of your spiritual life at present. Make some notes of this moment in time and how you are currently perceiving the spirit. This is valuable information to think about and becomes aware of before you venture into the unknown. The unknown scares almost every person. If it doesn't scare you, it certainly provides you with some sort of apprehensive emotion, regardless of how great or small. The unknown should be respected, acknowledged, and treated as the vast uncharted expanse that it is.

There is talk and many a tale of negative entities that roam the unknown lands beyond our own reach within the many religions and spiritual paths. These accounts have led to the rise in horror films such as The Exorcist. The media stretches most aspects of life until they are near to breaking point. As the media stands as a prominent educator within society, these horrors are thought or feared to be real.

Demonic entities, negative energies, and evil do exist. It exists within humanity, within the atrocities committed by people. Still, the saying "the devil made me do it" is nonsense. An entity cannot take over your mind or control you. It is you who allows this to happen if it ever happens. The line between psychic awareness and mental instability is a very fine one. Grounding, discussed in the previous chapter, assists with keeping things where they belong—in reality. You are a powerful spirit inhabiting a miraculous body controlling an awe-inspiring mind and steering your own ship. Nothing in this universe can take that power from you unless you allow it to happen.

How do people allow these things to occur because no person in their right mind would open their arms and permit a complete takeover by anything outside of themselves? You allow psychic attacks or negative influences to become part of your life when you decide to be dishonest in your life and take the road that will benefit only you. At the same time, you trample the world around you. You allow space for negativity when you live in filth or practice spirituality to control others. You give way to possession when you defile the spiritual laws of love and compassion. You bring disaster into your own life when you seek to cause pain and misfortune to something outside of yourself, or even yourself.

You are here to learn and then to teach and assist. Regardless of the path you follow, the career you have chosen, or the circumstances surrounding you, all you really have at the end of the day is your integrity. To want a connection with your spirit guide means that you have your word of honor. It means that in your heart, you are an honest person. It means that you are willing and are busy keeping to the spiritual laws ascribed to your soul. It also means that you will not use spirits for personal gain and control over those that come to you for aid. This does not mean that spiritual practitioners and masters may not charge for their services, for money is energy. Energy exchange is always a transaction regardless of what you are busy with. It means that you need to learn to become humble. You need to find your gratitude and remind yourself that you are that spec within the great ocean of all existence. It is only when you realize your inferiority within creation that you will gain your superiority within yourself. Not superiority over anything, but authority and power within.

When beginning your quest on the spiritual path, it is wise to ground and shield when not in session with your spirit guide. Shielding allows you to block the unwanted energies from the outside and provides you with a manner in which you can conserve your own state of being. For empaths who suffer greatly when entering crowded places, the act of shielding helps them immensely.

To shield, stand or sit quietly with your eyes closed. Visualize a golden light inside your solar plexus chakra. Allow this light to grow and resemble the sun. Enlarge the sunlight within you until this light surrounds you entirely. It should expand about a meter around your body, above and below you. Allow the light to swirl and dance around you. When you feel ready, visualize the most potent material you can think of, such as impenetrable titanium sheets. Pack these sheets or blocks of titanium around the sun that surrounds your body. Pack it closely together so that the light is only inside and none of it escapes. Then feel the security within this bubble. When you feel ready, surround this sun and titanium cocoon with an indigo-colored mist. The mist should be thick and heavy and surround the cocoon that you have built entirely. This indigo mist protects and shields you on the astral plane. When you have completed this visualization, you are ready for the day ahead.

When contacting or working with spirit, remember to repeat the meditation but do it in reverse this time, taking everything down and allowing the light to return to your solar plexus chakra. While doing spiritual work, an excellent visualization to replenish any lost energy is to pull that same light from the heavens or the sun itself. Visualize the energy from the sun traveling through the top of your head, filling every part of your body and eventually being condensed in your solar plexus region.

Your spirit guide will always protect you. Your connection with spirit will also always protect you. However, your own being needs to act following the spirit if you ask for that protection. It is the same as wanting to lose weight, but you scoff down twelve donuts for breakfast every day of your life with no exercise. The results will never be what you want them to be if you do not put in the effort. Everything is about balance. Everything is a case of giving and receiving. This is a world of duality. If we are to meander through the vast unknown, we need a guiding light. For that guiding light to reach us, we need to step into our own sacredness. We need to remember that we are more than the physical world, so much more.

Conclusion

Making contact with spirits within you and spirits without you leads to some of the most incredible experiences. This path is life-changing, and the mere request to come to know your spirit guide is a brilliant light on your way to positive transformation. There are many pitfalls along the path, many lessons, and many tears. Many dark nights of the soul that you will have to contend with and take into your stride. However, with the brutality of change, there is far more positivity to be experienced.

The sheer immensity of spiritual connection is not apparent in any language. There are no words or sentences to accurately explain the relationship with the spirit, and no experience is the same. Entire books have attempted to explain the process and the feeling that comes with walking the spiritual path. They have all fallen short of providing a holistic view. Why? Because your experience is never going to be the experience of someone else. You will never share the same perception of an ascended master as someone else does. You do not even taste food the same way, so why would your spiritual experiences be the same?

There are many people on the spiritual path who will offer

Conclusion

guidance and assistance. Some will have your best intentions at heart and others; will simply be seeking to make a quick dollar or two. It is part and parcel of the path to discerning which type of teacher these people are. When you find that someone you trusted is not who they seemed to be, remember that they came into your life for a reason. There is a lesson in this life at every turn. The benefit of walking the spiritual path is that you will always have a helping hand at your side, waiting to catch you when you trip and fall. There will always be someone to turn to, and you will never ever be alone again.

Connecting to spirit heals you from the inside out. It disrupts your entire being and takes your perception of the world, washes it, and places it back on you so that you can genuinely see with eyes of compassion, love, and grace. Walking the spiritual path is a necessity if you are to make contact with your spirit guide. It is a natural byproduct of the process. If you believe that you are simply going to meet your spirit guide once a week and then be done with it, think again. Spirit is contagious. Everything about the spiritual path and the thirst for more will drive you to dig deeper into the inner sanctums of religions. The more you search, the more you will learn about the things that you do not resonate with and know what to incorporate into your life.

There is, unfortunately, no hard cold truth to be found, except the truth of your own soul. There is no universal religion lying under the sands, waiting to be uncovered and save the planet. There is only your own healing and enlightening journey waiting to be explored. There is also no concrete answer in any book on this earth. Each book holds a sentence of truth for your soul, or a passage or perhaps many parts of the book, but no truth will be your truth. If you find this happening, pray about it because the mind looks for ways to cotton onto and copy ways that seem more beneficial for our own survival. The truth will dissipate eventually, and you will be back on your own path. It is best to remain completely

Conclusion

honest with yourself at all times, removing any decision-making through fear or guilt, or pity.

The world is your oyster and not your hospital. It is not your responsibility to heal the planet, find the solution to world peace or reinvent the wheel. As messed up as most of the planet seems, there is a fundamental reason for everything to be as it is. If you follow your own inner compass, you can never go wrong. It is with you because that is your proverbial GPS set to the coordinates of your absolute success. You are far more powerful, wise, and beautiful than you understand. By making the decision to make contact with your spirit guide, you have opened the door to a world of great adventure and learning. May it be a soul-completing process, and may you always find the reason for joy and self-compassion, even in the darkest corners of life.

References

American Psychological Association. (2006, March 20). Multitasking: Switching costs. APA.org. https://www.apa.org/research/action/multitask

askAstrology. (n.d.). Numerology: Meanings, Name, Life Path, Calculator, Reading. AskAstrology. https://askastrology.com/numerology/

Cheiro. (1971). The Cheiro book of fate and fortune: palmistry, numerology, astrology. London, Barrie And Jenkins.

Chevalier, G., Sinatra, S. T., Oschman, J. L., Sokal, K., & Sokal, P. (2012). Earthing: Health Implications of Reconnecting the Human Body to the Earth's Surface Electrons. Journal of Environmental and Public Health, 2012, 1–8. https://doi.org/10.1155/2012/291541

Crowley, B., & Crowley, E. (1994). Words of power : sacred sounds of East and West. Llewellyn.

EBFAFitness. (2018, June 28). The Anti Aging Effects of Earthing with Dr Emily Splichal. YouTube. https://www.youtube.com/watch?v=hs_UQA2uC9A

Esselmont, B. (2018). Tarot Card Meanings. Biddy Tarot. https://www.biddytarot.com/tarot-card-meanings

Griffin, W. (1995). The Embodied Goddess: Feminist

References

Witchcraft and Female Divinity. Sociology of Religion, 56(1), 35-49. https://web.csulb.edu/~wgriffin/embodied.html

Harvard Health Publishing. (2011). Giving thanks can make you happier. Healthbeat; Harvard Health Publishing. https://www.health.harvard.edu/healthbeat/giving-thanks-can-make-you-happier

Harvard Health Publishing. (2019, June 5). In Praise of Gratitude. Harvard Mental Health Letter. Harvard Health Publishing. https://www.health.harvard.edu/mind-and-mood/in-praise-of-gratitude

Herbert, F., & Herbert, B. (2019). Dune. Ace Books.

Hermes, T., M Doreal, & Temple. (2002). The emerald tablets of Thoth-the-Atlantean: a literal translation of one of the most ancient and secret of the great works of the ancient wisdom. Brotherhood Of The White Temple.

Illes, J. (2009). Encyclopedia of spirits: the ultimate guide to the magic of saints, angels, fairies, demons, and ghosts. Harperone.

Illes, J. (2011). Encyclopedia of mystics, saints & sages: a guide to asking for protection, wealth, happiness, and everything else! Harperone.

Johnson, S. (2001). The Gospel of Yeshua : a fresh look at the life and teaching of Jesus. Corinthian Books.

Kaku, Dr. M. (n.d.-a). Blackholes, Wormholes and the Tenth Dimension. Dr. Michio Kaku. https://mkaku.org/home/articles/blackholes-wormholes-and-the-tenth-dimension/

Kaku, Dr. M. (n.d.-b). Official Website of Dr. Michio Kaku. https://mkaku.org/

Lal-Singh, L. (2016, January 26). Lord Melchizedek. The Ascended Masters - Their Work and Purpose. http://theascendedmasters.com/lord-melchizedek/

Laurie-Elle. (2019). Channels, Spirit Guides, Higher Self & Etheric Cords. Our Sight Your Light. https://www.oursightyourlight.com/blog/channels-angels-spiritguides

References

Lee, L., Roser, M., & Ortiz-Ospina, E. (2015). Suicide. Our World in Data. https://ourworldindata.org/suicide

Lightman, A. (2018, April 6). Fact and Faith: why science and spirituality are not incompatible. Science Focus. BBC Science Focus Magazine. https://www.sciencefocus.com/the-human-body/fact-and-faith-why-science-and-spirituality-are-not-incompatible/

Lotto, B. (n.d.). Beau Lotto. Beau Lotto. https://www.beaulotto.com/

Lotto, B. (2017). Deviate. Orion Publishing Group.

Merriam-Webster. (n.d.). Psychic. In Merriam-Webster.com dictionary. https://www.merriam-webster.com/dictionary/psychic

Merriam-Webster. (2019). Trust. In Merriam-Webster.com dictionary. https://www.merriam-webster.com/dictionary/trust

Myss, C. (2020). Caroline Myss. Caroline Myss. https://www.myss.com/

New King James Version Bible. (1984). Biblia. https://biblia.com/bible/nkjv/luke/1/29-30

Norman, R., & Spaegel, C. (1988). Ra-Mu of Lemuria speaks: transmissions from the Unarius Brothers class student testimonials and healings. Unarius Educational Foundation.

Of The Cross, J., Avila, T., & E Allison Peers. (2009). The complete works of Saint John of the Cross, doctor of the Church. Kessinger.

Of, F., & Backhouse, H. C. (1994). The writings of St Francis of Assisi. Hodder & Stoughton.

Peterson, C. (2008, May 16). What Is Positive Psychology, and What Is It Not? Psychology Today. https://www.psychologytoday.com/za/blog/the-good-life/200805/what-is-positive-psychology-and-what-is-it-not

Prophet, M., Prophet, E. C., & Booth, A. (2003). The masters and their retreats. Summit University Press.

Radford, B. (2018, March 30). Are Angels Real?. Live

References

Science. https://www.livescience.com/26071-are-angels-real.html

Reeves, R. R., Ladner, M. E., Hart, R. H., & Burke, R. S. (2007). Nocebo effects with antidepressant clinical drug trial placebos. General Hospital Psychiatry, 29(3), 275–277. https://doi.org/10.1016/j.genhosppsych.2007.01.010

Lexico Dictionaries. (2019). Religion in Lexico Dictionaries. https://www.lexico.com/definition/religion

Richardson, T. (2061). Angel Insights. Llewellyn Worldwide.

Rorem, P., & Pontifical Institute Of Mediaeval Studies. (2005). Eriugena's commentary on the Dionysian Celestial hierarchy. Pontifical Institute Of Mediaeval Studies.

Schutte, S. (2009, January 1). Trusting: Let God Do the Driving. Focus on the Family. https://www.focusonthefamily.com/faith/trusting-let-god-do-the-driving/

Spirit guide. (2020, July 28). In Wikipedia. https://en.wikipedia.org/wiki/Spirit_guide

"Spiritual Guide." (n.d.). In Encyclopedia of Religion. https://www.encyclopedia.com/environment/encyclopedias-almanacs-transcripts-and-maps/spiritual-guide

Splichal, E. (2017). Meet the Doctor. Dr Emily Splichal DPM. https://www.dremilysplichal.com/meet-the-doctor

Swan, T. (2019, February 19). Spirit Animals (What Is Your Spirit Animal and How To Find Your Spirit Animal). Teal Swan. https://tealswan.com/videos/spirituality/spirit-animals-what-is-your-spirit-animal-and-how-to-find-your-spirit-animal-r362/

Swan, T. (2021). Teal Swan. Teal Swan; Teal Eye LLC. https://tealswan.com/

The Book of Enoch: Enoch's Journeys through the Earth and Sheol: Chapter XX. (n.d.). Sacred Texts. https://www.sacred-texts.com/bib/boe/boe023.htm

The Tibetan lama who was really a plumber from Devon. (2020, May 17). The Guardian. https://www.theguardian.-

References

com/travel/2020/may/17/tibetan-lama-who-was-a-plumber-from-devon-1956-bestseller-the-third-eye

University of Pennsylvania. (2011). Martin E.P. Seligman. Positive Psychology Center. https://ppc.sas.upenn.edu/people/martin-ep-seligman

Wigington, P. (2019, November 27). 10 Basic Divination Methods to Try. Learn Religions. https://www.learnreligions.com/methods-of-divination-2561764

Yogananda, P. (2008). Whispers from eternity. Self Realization Fellowship.

About the Author

Monique Joiner Siedlak is a writer, witch, and warrior on a mission to awaken people to their greatest potential through the power of storytelling infused with mysticism, modern paganism, and new age spirituality. At the young age of 12, she began rigorously studying the fascinating philosophy of Wicca. By the time she was 20, she was self-initiated into the craft, and hasn't looked back ever since. To this day, she has authored over 40 books pertaining to the magick and mysteries of life.

To find out more about Monique Joiner Siedlak artistically, spiritually, and personally, feel free to visit her **official website**.

www.mojosiedlak.com

facebook.com/mojosiedlak
twitter.com/mojosiedlak
instagram.com/mojosiedlak
pinterest.com/mojosiedlak
bookbub.com/authors/monique-joiner-siedlak

More Books by Monique

African Spirituality Beliefs and Practices
Hoodoo
Seven African Powers: The Orishas
Cooking for the Orishas
Lucumi: The Ways of Santeria
Voodoo of Louisiana
Haitian Vodou
Orishas of Trinidad
Connecting With Your Ancestors
Blood Magic
The Orishas

Practical Magick
Wiccan Basics
Candle Magick
Wiccan Spells
Love Spells
Abundance Spells
Herb Magick
Moon Magick
Creating Your Own Spells

More Books by Monique

Gypsy Magic
Protection Magick
Celtic Magick

Get a Handle on Life
Stress Management
Get a Handle on Anxiety
Get a Handle on Depression
Get a Handle on Procrastination

Divination Magic for Beginners
Divination with Runes: A Beginner's Guide to Rune Casting

The Yoga Collective
Yoga for Beginners
Yoga for Stress
Yoga for Back Pain
Yoga for Weight Loss
Yoga for Flexibility
Yoga for Advanced Beginners
Yoga for Fitness
Yoga for Runners
Yoga for Energy
Yoga for Your Sex Life
Yoga to Beat Depression and Anxiety
Yoga for Menstruation
Yoga to Detox Your Body
Yoga to Tone Your Body

A Natural Beautiful You
Creating Your Own Body Butter
Creating Your Own Body Scrub
Creating Your Own Body Spray

Last Chance Join My Newsletter!

If you missed it, I have a free gift available for you and wanted to remind you it's still available.

mojosiedlak.com/self-help-and-yoga-newsletter

Thank you for reading my book.
I really appreciate all your feedback and would love to hear what you have to say!
Please leave your review at your favorite retailer!

www.ingramcontent.com/pod-product-compliance
Lightning Source LLC
Chambersburg PA
CBHW061331040426
42444CB00011B/2857